PRAISE FOR
GET IT ON!

"If you are a veteran, you need to read this book. Keni Thomas has worn the boots. He is a patriot. He is one of us. His story is gripping. His faith is ispiring. Keni shows us that the principles of leadership we learned when we wore the uniform still apply to us all out here in the real world. It is through the example we set, and by the grace of God that we can still make a difference and continue to live purposeful and meaningful lives."

　　　　　　　　　　　　—LtCol Oliver L. North, USMC (Retired)

"Based on his combat experiences with Task Force Ranger, *Get It On!* is a how-to manual that applies the psychology of his elite special operations training to the challenges of every day life in the real world. Keni believes that with God's grace, we all have the power to effectively make a difference. I have witnessed his words in action as he leads the way by his personal example, supporting the children of his fallen comrades through The Special Operations Warrior Foundation."

　　　　　—General Peter J. Schoomaker, 35th Chief of Staff of the Army

"Keni Thomas is the real deal. His experiences at the heart of the Battle of Mogadishu taught him about a lot more than the tactics and methods of an elite soldier. Here he has created an engaging and inspiring tutorial, applying those lessons to the battles of everyday life, which are rarely as intense, but usually last a lot longer than a firefight."

　　　　　　　　　　　—Mark Bowden, author of *Black Hawk Down*

"Keni's selfless efforts to give back to our men and women in uniform are a testament to his message of setting an example for others to follow. The leadership principles Keni shares through his story *Get It On!* are directly aligned with the core values of our organization. To Lead is to Serve. The USO is proud to call Keni Thomas one of our own."

—Sloan Gibson, President of the USO

"Over the course of the last six years, Keni and I have proudly joined forces in support of the Special Operations Warrior Foundation. He is a tireless crusader, who walks the path he preaches. *Get It On!* is a moving account of courage and faith under fire. True leadership is about the example we set. Keni has an impressive way of convincing you that this is a principle we should all live by"

—Hal Steinbrenner, owner of the New York Yankees

"Keni Thomas is a captivating speaker and an inspiring story teller who has now given us a book just as engaging. *Get It On!* uses his personal story of survival on the battlefield to show us how we all matter and we can indeed make an impact on the world around us."

—David Horowitz, political activist and founder of the Freedom Center

GET IT ON!

WHAT IT MEANS TO LEAD THE WAY

U.S. ARMY RANGERS VETERAN OF "BLACK HAWK DOWN" MISSION

KENI THOMAS

RBM
PUBLISHING

978-1-4336-7274-3

Published by RBM Publishing
Nashville, Tennessee

Dewey Decimal Classification: 303.3
Subject Heading: LEADERSHIP \ THOMAS, KENI \
CHRISTIAN LIFE

8 • 20 19 18 17 16 15

Thank you God for using me and for sending me,
to do what I love. I am so very grateful you have stuck
with me. And to the men of Task Force Ranger,
who fought to bring each other home. Thank you for giving
me the chance to live the dream. I am forever indebted to you.

ACKNOWLEDGMENTS

EVER SINCE I WAS A kid I've been rehearsing my acceptance speech at the Grammys.

Now I know why the producers have to start playing that stupid music to cut you off. If you thanked everyone that had a hand in your success, you'd be there all night.

So you thank the ones you love like your family, Cris, Claire, and Duane Ward. You thank the ones who believed in the beginning like Gary and Esther. You thank the crew and the cast over at LifeWay/B&H Publishing Group like Julie Gwinn, John Thompson, Jeff Godby, and the countless others who lent their talents to this project. You give special thanks to that unique individual who guided you through the process of creation and kept you motivated when you would rather have quit. That someone would be AJ. And finally you thank God for bringing all these folks into your life and placing them on your left and on your right.

As you walk away with award in hand, you wave to the crowd and thank the fans! Because without you, I'm just talking to myself.

CONTENTS

Introduction 1

Chapter 1: Get It On! 7

Chapter 2: The Posse 19

Chapter 3: Train as You Fight. Fight as You Train. 37

Chapter 4: Ropes 51

Chapter 5: Lead, Follow, or Get Out of the Way 75

Chapter 6: Hollywood 101

Chapter 7: The Medic and the Machine Gunner
and other Angels of War 119

Chapter 8: The Long Night .141

Chapter 9: The Mile 163

Chapter 10: Extraordinary Individuals 191

Chapter 11: RLTW 207

The Ranger Creed 221

INTRODUCTION

MAN THIS WAS GETTING CRAZY. Todd Blackburn just fell out of the helicopter during insertion and somebody got shot while trying to help him. But none of us knew for sure because Chalk 4 wasn't where they were supposed to be. They roped-in a block too soon.

It was getting chaotic. People were shooting at us. Somalis were showing up everywhere, running back and forth across the streets like those little moving targets at the shooting arcade in Frontierland at Disney. *Should we fire at them?* Some had weapons. Some did not. It was hard to tell. But somebody had to be shooting at us from the corners of those buildings because a lot of Rangers were firing back in all directions, and rules of engagement say we don't fire unless there's someone firing at us.

Even the helicopters overhead were engaged. The bone-rattling roar of their mini-guns sounded like slow-motion lightning ripping the sky apart. There's a terrible sense of urgency forced through your nerves when those fully automatic Gatling guns let loose at a total annihilation rate of 10,000 rounds per minute.

Who are they firing at? Are there really that many bad guys out there? Man, what's happening? Thirty minutes ago I was in shorts and flip-flops writing a letter home to my mom. I think they call this being in combat. What was that? I think I just got hit. So this is what it feels like.

I was kneeling against the wall of the target building, which is exactly where they tell you NOT to kneel because bullets follow walls. How would someone know this? Who tested that theory? Must have been someone just like me who leaned against a wall and then got hit by a wall-following bullet. But it's an instinctive thing to run for cover. So when there really isn't any cover out in a street, you run for a wall. You lean against it because it just feels more secure, right up until some Somali from two hundred yards down the road fires a burst from his AK-47 in your general direction and the trajectory path of those rounds begin hurtling toward you at 715 meters per sec. Good news is, the person who pulled the trigger was not very disciplined, so the bullets are off target and are going to miss their mark, me, and instead slam into the wall about five feet in front of me. Bad news is, the rounds continue their forward velocity, skipping off the wall and impacting center mass at original said target: me. Lucky shot.

On the receiving end it's hard to believe a tiny little thing like a bullet could hit you with so much force. If you've ever had Derek Jeter swing a baseball bat into your midsection and knock you backwards on your butt, then you know exactly what it's like to get struck by a couple of wall-skipping 7.62 rounds. If you haven't had Derek Jeter do that to you, then take my word for it, bullets pack a punch. One hit me solidly in the ammo pouch and was stopped by one of the ammunition magazines, which is only about an inch wide. I fell back on my butt and thought I was going to explode. Literally.

The rounds in my magazine were smoking from the impact. In my confusion, I'm thinking they might start cooking off or something. So I started yanking the ammunition out of my pouch like hot potatoes. Apparently, the sight must have been funny to see, because my buddy Randy Ramaglia was across the street laughing at me. Another round went through the ammo pouch, destroyed a magazine, and exited out the back bouncing off my Kevlar plate. "Thank God for body armor."

It would take me many battles and many years to understand the full meaning of those words. In the big scheme of that particular day in history, me getting hit by two poorly aimed and ricocheting 7.62mm rounds was just a small inconsequential moment, one I don't even bother to talk about when I tell the story of that day. One man being "almost hurt" is rather unmentionable given 78 others were wounded and 19 killed. But as I have grown in my faith through the years, I have come to realize it was not the body armor that saved me. It was God's armor and the extraordinary men He placed on my left and right. He had a job for me to do later down the line and wanted me to make it out.

"The LORD your God is in your midst, a
victorious warrior." (Zephaniah 3:17 NASB)

The physical wounds of a combat veteran will heal in time. But there are some scars that never go away. When you walk away from something others did not, you will spend the rest of your life thanking those people who were on your left and on your right that day. Because I know the only reason I am still here today is by the grace of God and the efforts of those men. I will honor them both by proudly telling our story to all who will listen.

You will also find yourself forever struggling and haunted by an odd sense of guilt. Why me, God? Why did You let me live when others, did not? Men who had families. Men who were three times the soldier I was. People who deserved to live. So why me?

You can let the guilt do one of two things. It can bury you in anger and pity. Or you can use it to motivate you to live up to everything you're worth. Knowing your worth and realizing just how important you are to the big picture is a challenge and something I struggle with even today.

Most of us want to make a difference in this world. We want to know at the end of the day that we matter, that we counted for something. Those who wear the uniform of the U.S. military need not worry about that. But for the rest of us out here in the real world we wonder, "How do *I* make a difference?" "What can *I* do that really matters?" "How will *I* be remembered?"

My friends, these are easy questions to answer if all you do is lead and lead by example. Because when you set an example for others to follow, those around you take notice. I promise you they do. Whether they tell you or not, they are watching. You lead, they will follow, and the team around you becomes stronger. Thus, you have made a difference and you have changed a life.

The Army manual on Military Leadership FM-22-100 has a simple definition for leadership: *Leadership is the Process of influencing others to accomplish the mission by providing purpose, direction, and motivation.* It is a simple explanation, but exactly how you go about providing the purpose, direction, and motivation necessary to influence others is a topic that can fill thousands of books and millions of pages. I'm certainly not here to write another lesson on *how* to be a better leader. I just want you to be one.

I realize most of us do not actually hold a position of leadership. Notice at no point does the definition of leadership say anything about, rank, seniority, status, tenure, hierarchy, pay-grade, pecking order, totem poles, or ducks in a row. Remember it's never the title or the position that defines a great leader. It is the example you set. The Wizard of Oz didn't give anything to the lion he didn't already have.

The people who fill the pages of this book are not the generals, colonels, or captains. They are the brand new sergeants like Randy Ramaglia who took over for his squad when his squad leader went down. They are the young privates like David Floyd. He was in charge of no one but himself, but the example he set was exceptional. He saved my life and those around him.

When Paul the apostle sat alone for years in a Roman cell, he had some time on his hands. Instead of feeling sorry for himself, he used that time to do some good. He wrote a whole bunch of letters to folks who needed guidance on how to move forward with this new thing called Christianity. In the most famous part of his letter to the Ephesians, he advises them to suit up for battle. "Put on all of God's armor so that you will be able to stand firm against all strategies of the devil [or enemy]" (Eph. 6:11 NLT).

To help illustrate the reality of spiritual warfare, Paul used the modern-day battlefield of the Roman Empire to make his point. As will I. Because whether we are talking about the conquest of Germania, the Russian front, the beaches of Normandy, the mountains of Korea, the jungles of Vietnam, the streets of Mogadishu, Bagdad, or Kabul, the stories told by those who were there carry a common theme. Somebody, somewhere, at some terribly urgent moment and against all odds, did something extraordinary to lead the way. They set an example for others to follow. Be that person.

I can't tell you where. I can't tell you when. But I can tell you with absolute certainty the call *will* come for you to get it on! And just like that, the course of your life will change forever. Will you be prepared? Will you have what it takes to *"readily display the intestinal fortitude required to fight on to the Ranger objective and complete the mission, though I be the lone survivor?"* Of course you will. Why? Because you are a *"specially selected and well-trained soldier"* with a promise to keep—*"never shall I fail my comrades."*

You understand what it means to be counted on and are willing to carry the burden of leadership that can be a heavy load to bear at times. That's why so many shy away from the responsibility. They don't want to do the hard work of leadership. Being counted on means you might fail, so it's much easier not to try. But you are not that person. You have purpose. You have direction. And you are motivated to "Lead the way, all the way."

This is the story of extraordinary people just like you who did just that.

The men of Chalk 3 and the crew of the Gunslinger call sign Super 66—Top: Mike Kurth, Sean Watson, Stan Wood, Gary Fuller, Richard Strous, Eric Suranski, me, and George Siegler. Bottom: David Floyd, Ned "No Fear" Norton, Jeffrey Hulst, Scott Hargis, John Collette, and Melvin Dejesus.

Chapter 1

GET IT ON!

*I will always endeavor to uphold the prestige, honor,
and high esprit de corps of my Ranger Regiment.*
—1ST STANZA OF THE RANGER CREED

THREE WORDS. THAT'S ALL IT took. I was writing a letter home to my mom when the call rang out across the American compound. "Get it on!" And just like that, the course of my life was changed forever.

A mission was coming down and it was time to gear up. Like firefighters running for their coats and helmets or fighter pilots scrambling to their jets, men dropped what they were doing and hustled toward their weapons to begin the transformation from soldier to superman.

Dear Mom, Hope all is well at home. I'll have to finish this letter a little later. We just got a call. Nothing to worry about. Probably a false alarm. Love, Keni.

I was wrong. Fifteen minutes later I was locked and loaded and on board an MH-60 Black Hawk screaming along the African coastline en route to a target building deep in the war-torn heart of Mogadishu, Somalia. A report came in over the headset that heavy weapons were spotted on the objective. We were going in hot. I sat in the open door, knees to the breeze, with the Indian Ocean gleaming beneath me in the late afternoon sun. As the shadow of the helicopter glided off the turquoise water, up over the dingy beach, and into the urban sprawl of the third-world slums below, the thoughts I enjoyed just moments before of home in Florida and Mom's pecan pie were a lifetime away.

We knew going in it was a dangerous part of town. We knew there were bad guys waiting for us on the objective. We knew a daylight raid was an increased risk. What we didn't know is by the time it was all done, nineteen of us would never make it back and another seventy-eight would be wounded. Even the fortunate minority who did not get shot, fragmented, or blown up would forever carry the emotional scars that are standard issue for the combat veteran. The body will heal itself in time. The heart and mind take a whole lot longer.

Three words were all it took to get me there. I've spent the rest of my life trying to figure out why God pulled me out.

"The army taught me some great lessons—
to be prepared for catastrophe—to endure
being bored—and to know that however fine a
fellow I thought myself in my usual routine, there
were other situations . . . in which I was inferior
to men that I might have looked down upon had
not experience taught me to look up."
(Oliver Wendell Holmes Jr.)

It was supposed to have been a day off for the men of Task Force Ranger. We had been in Somalia for almost three months going non-stop day and night. If we weren't running a mission into the city, then we were busy training for one. Here it was October and finally we were catching a break. It was good to hear the boys laughing and enjoying the afternoon. Some of them were outside playing volleyball. Some were doing whatever it is they do on their downtime to kill time.

The military is full of all walks of life. You get some pretty squared away people who become your best friends. But there's also those stereotypically strange individuals who, on their day off, would prefer to sit in the shadows sharpening knives for hours at a time. Good thing they were on our side. You don't have to like everyone you work with. You just have to count on them.

I climbed on top of a big storage connex to find some real estate to call my own. Seclusion is a pipe dream when you live with four hundred men in an airplane hangar. From up there I could at least enjoy the breeze coming in off the ocean. The Mogadishu Airport was less than a mile from the coast. Thank God, because without the wind, the air smelled like crap. Literally. The nasty, stinking porta-potties were baking in the heat. But, if you closed your eyes and forgot where you really were, it wasn't so hard to imagine being home on the Florida coast, where right about now, my friends were probably on their way to the beach or church, it being Sunday and all.

It felt like a small victory to enjoy the sun rather than curse it as we usually did while training out in the sand dunes. The African heat will put a hurtin' on you when dressed in full battle uniform. But for now, the first sergeant relaxed just a little on our dress code so most of us were hanging around in our PT uniforms of shorts and T-shirts.

Be nice if I could take my shirt off, I thought. But I knew First Sergeant Glenn Harris still wasn't going to let us go "all Hollywood" like the Delta operators and flight crews in their Oakley sunglasses and Teva flip-flops. You can take the Ranger away from Regiment, but you can't take Regiment away from the Ranger.

Other than the weather, there was very little to like about this place. You would think being on a beach might be enjoyable. It might have been, except the beach was strictly off limits. This wasn't for security reasons or a fear of some random Somali attack while we were in the water. The rule was in place due to an entirely different threat—sharks.

About a mile down shore was an old meat processing plant where the Somalis used to butcher cattle and dump the remains into the water. If you're a shark, hey, free food. But when the supply of dead cow stopped coming, the predators turned to slow humans. One Russian soldier was killed. Another U.N. peacekeeper lost a bite-size portion of her hip. So no beach for us.

It didn't matter if we were allowed to go swimming or not. We rarely had time to ourselves, except at the end of the day before lights out. That's when we would return to our cots to write letters, read books, listen to music, play board games, or maybe go to the TV room and watch movies. We had a box of tapes and a VCR. But how many times can you watch *Platoon*? Quiet time to ourselves is a place when a soldier starts thinking about something other than soldiering. Home. *How's my family? Wonder what my friends are doing? Wonder how she's doing?* Suddenly those somewhat average evenings on the couch watching a movie at my girlfriend's house sure seem a lot more wonderful now. *God, I miss her.*

Sometimes, if we were lucky, we had a letter to read or a package to open. Mail call for a soldier is a bit of a magic moment. When something arrives with your name on it via the U.S. mail, it feels like your own personal Christmas, only with more meaning. When you're stuck out in some remote godforsaken chunk of the world, as soldiers always are, it's easy to think no one back home remembers you. A letter with your name on it meant someone still cared. It meant you weren't forgotten. It was your one link to the magical place we once knew called *home*. I was fortunate. I got a lot of letters, so I would spread the love and share them with my buddies.

I think the reason I got more mail than most was because I knew a lot of girls. I'm not sure if it's been documented or not, but it's a well-known fact girls are much better at writing letters than guys. If you write to a girl, she'll usually write you back. You see how that works?

We didn't have cell phones and e-mail back then, so if you wanted to receive, you had to give. You had to make an effort. Find a piece of paper and the preferred writing instrument of your choice. A pencil or pen for most. A crayon for some. And then, here's the hard part, convert your thoughts into actual sentences and write them down. Sign your name, fold the letter up, put it in an envelope, write an address on it, seal it up, buy a stamp, lick it, stick it, walk it to the mail box, and drop it in the slot. And then you wait. Waiting is something a soldier is very adept at doing.

The only real excitement going on around the compound was the occasional mortar attack. The first couple times it was a bit unsettling. For a split second you hear the incoming round ripping through the air. Then you feel its impact followed by the sound of the explosion. Everyone would grab their gear and run for a bunker. The randomness of where the rounds might land was not a gamble I liked having to make. It was like an old lady pumping nickels into a slot machine. Sooner or later she's gonna hit one. I didn't want to be the jackpot for some Somali insurgent and his mortar tube.

By about the third time we got mortared, we somehow got used to the ordeal. It became more of a hassle than a threat. I realized there wasn't a thing you could do about it, so what was the point in fearing it? Eventually, it got to where guys began to cheer when a random mortar round would explode somewhere in our vicinity. I'm not kidding you. They cheered. There was even a mortar betting pool where you could wager on how many rounds would land and on what day. For the soldier doing time in a combat zone, humor is good cover and concealment from reality.

"And each man stands with his face in the light of his own drawn sword. Ready to do what a hero can." (Elizabeth Barrett Browning)

The call to *"Get it on"* was always welcomed, and I'm sure you can see why. Like a lifeguard secretly hoping someone starts to drown, it meant perhaps this time we would finally get the chance to do what we came here to do. What we trained to do. What we enlisted to do. What we thought about doing our entire lives since we were kids playing army, running around the streets of our neighborhoods shooting at each other with sticks, dirt clogs, and bottle rockets.

Wanting to fight lies in the heart of every man since boyhood. Thank God, because where would we be without those very same boys who we have trained and sent to do the dirty work of the real world? War is a terrible and unfortunate reality, but it is as much a part of mankind as fire and rain. Both can be beneficial. Both can be ultimately destructive.

The point is, without warriors willing to stand up and be sent, the world would be ruled by the wicked and ill-intended. We were born into a world at war. Before any of us even drew a living breath on this planet, there was good and there was evil. Both are fighting for your very soul. The fight has always been here. But somewhere along the line of raising a boy into a man, the obscurity of moral correctness gradually concocts itself into a confusing cloud of ambiguity. Society, school, church, friends, the opinions of scholars, or your mother divorced from a combat veteran who chose duty over family, begin to remold your conscience, which tells you wanting to go fight is wrong. It's a bad thing and you are screwed up for wanting to do so.

As a soldier, you ignore those "voices of morality." You learn to embrace the role of the warrior and its social outcast image. So you speak with comical rhetoric using tough guy one-liners to reinforce the triviality of death—"Kill something everyday no matter how small, just to stay proficient" or one of my favorites, "You can run, but you'll only die tired." We name ourselves "devil dogs" and "Night Stalkers." "Hunter/killer teams" always sounded better to me than "reconnaissance."

From day one of basic training, the soldier sings "Hooah, hooah!" and callous cadences about the honorable destruction of the enemy. Call him "the enemy" and he's no longer human. Say it enough and you'll begin to believe it. You have to desensitize yourself because, if you don't, your conscience will tear you apart and you'll become combat ineffective. You will be incapable of doing whatever needs to be done at the time it needs doing. So the warrior must hide the good boy that society expects of him and become the hard man the nation needs him to be—a highly trained, highly motivated, and highly effective killer of men.

This is why we used a lot of humor about ourselves. It was a way to mask our "socially unacceptable" enthusiasm for what we really hoped for, the call to "get it on." Though it may very well be screwed up, we wanted the real deal, the chance to pull the trigger and get "the enemy" we were after. Besides, the sooner we got the job done, the sooner we could get out of this hole and back to America, the land of hot showers, our own bed, real toilets, wives, kids, and girlfriends.

"Get it on!"

I tucked the letter to my mom away and hustled to the hangar toward my cot where my gear was stowed. I pulled the desert-patterned BDU pants up over my PT shorts, buttoned the blouse, laced on the boots, and started gearing up. All around me men were doing the same, strapping on body armor, slinging equipment, checking weapon systems, and mentally transitioning from volleyball to combat. Some guys were joking with the usual sarcasm that "this was gonna be the big one." Some guys said nothing at all.

Whatever the outside appearance of these soldiers may have been, I can tell you with certainty what was going on inside. The mental roller coaster we put ourselves through was in full swing. One afternoon you are on your own time thinking like a son, a father, or a husband of life back home. Then suddenly you are called to action and, just like that, you are expected to transform into a combat professional, concentrating only on the immediate task at hand.

Your brain begins to pump adrenaline into your system. Your mind starts racing through your job responsibilities, tactics, mission parameters, combat scenarios, and other life and death matters. All the while, you're hoping this time will indeed "be the big one," but you never let yourself get too excited because more often than not, it'll end up being a false alarm. In fact, that very same morning we were alerted, geared up, and made it as far as the aircraft, only to be told the mission was a "no go." "Oh well, back to playing volleyball."

Being alerted was a fairly common occurrence. Since the Somali militia already knew we were there, the idea was to keep them guessing as to when we were coming. Sometimes we would simply fly around the city in what was called "signature flights." Sometimes we would do false insertions. Every now and then there was a real live confirmed target and the mission was a go. But you never *really* knew until the last minute. Combat has always rightly been described as long periods of boredom interrupted by instantaneous chaos.

Even though the call to arms was becoming routine, it was crucial you never took the routine for granted. Like a firefighter on duty at the station, sooner or later the call is going to come. Can't tell you when. Can't tell you where. But it's going to come. And when it does, you better be ready. In his haste to get out the door and rush to the emergency, you can imagine how easy it might be for the firefighter to forget something important like his oxygen tank or an IV bag. The true professional, however, does not make that kind of mistake, because he knows if you start taking routine for granted, it leads to something called complacency.

I don't care what it is you do for a living; complacency is going to cause issues. And in the business of combat, those issues cost lives. Do not assume just because it was right the last time, it will automatically be right again. Always do your double checks.

"Don't Forget Nothing!" (Captain Robert Rogers)

There was a man named Robert Rogers who is generally considered to be the very first Ranger. He and his men fought in the pre-revolutionary French and Indian wars of the American frontier. Captain Rogers had a very practical list of standing orders, appropriately called Rogers' Rangers Standing Orders. They were an absolute given for all his men. Even the Rangers today are required to know them. The very first thing on that list was "Don't forget nothing." Excellent combat advice if poor English.

Once everyone gathered their gear, it was my job as a team leader to line my men up and make sure we had everything we were supposed to have as a squad. Every person had a job to do and every job depended on the other. So in heeding Capt. Rogers' orders and to ensure nothing necessary was forgotten, we all had to double-check each other. Does the machine gunner have all his extra rounds? Is the gun bubble-wrapped to keep the dirt out on infill? Is the medical bag packed to standard?

Some of the guys carried explosives like C-4, which is a Play-Doh-like substance that can be molded and shaped to fit just about any of your demolition needs. By itself C-4 is harmless. It takes two things to make it explode, heat and pressure. This is usually accomplished by a tiny firecracker device called a blasting cap. You jam it into the Play-Doh and send an electric current to the blasting cap.

Doesn't take much of a charge either. A 9-volt battery is all you need. The blasting cap explodes, causing heat and pressure, which in turn detonates the C-4 and *KABOOM!* Your door is blown down or the wall you want to go through now has a hole in it. Since all I had was young guys who were prone to make mistakes, it was very important to me to ensure one of my guys did not pick up the blasting caps and put them in the same bag with the C-4. *KABOOM* in that case is not good.

Our basic load weighed about fifty pounds including the body armor and weapon. Some guys had even more to carry depending on their particular assignment. At times a Ranger feels a lot like a pack mule, only he's expected to move as quick as a racehorse. In addition to my rifle and basic load of grenades and ammo, I also carried a sawed-off Remington shotgun I Velcroed to my hip and a rocket launcher called a LAW (light anti-tank weapon). It was a small extendable tube I hated carrying mostly because it added another four and a half pounds, which was just enough to make my knees begin to buckle.

I remember asking my platoon sergeant Sergeant First Class Sean T. Watson, "Hey, S'rgnt Watson. Why do I have to carry this thing? They don't have any tanks." He fired back a one-liner that could only have come from a man with years of experience and a lot more rank than me. "Because, Sgt. Thomas, it's better to have and not need, than to need and not have. I might need it, but I'm not carrying it. So you will." Good combat advice.

The only thing we knew for sure we would not need is our night vision devices and water. Since this mission wouldn't take much more than an hour, we'd be back long before dark. So why carry the extra weight?

Now I'm sure Captain Rogers came about his standing orders by years of hard lessons learned and many lives lost. If "*don't forget nothing*" was his very first and therefore most important point to make, you would think we Rangers would have listened more carefully. We keep relearning what history has tried so hard to teach us again and again.

> Don't forget nothing. It is better to have and not need, than to need and not have.

When you heed a lesson, it's a good thing. When you find yourself relearning a lesson, it's usually a bad thing. I would live them both in just a few short hours.

Heading into the city flying low over the rooftops.

Chapter 2

THE POSSE

*Gallantly will I show the world that I am a specially
selected and well-trained soldier.*
—4TH STANZA OF THE RANGER CREED

MUHAMMED FARRAH AIDEED WAS A bad man. He and his clan
of *Habr Gidir* militia had been attacking the United Nations food
shipments. A haven for terrorists and warlords, Somalia was a country
whose very existence was threatened by civil war, particularly
through the violent efforts of a political bully like Aideed. In the early
1990s the United Nations was supplying the chaotic African nation
with humanitarian aid because of the civil war and the starvation
crisis destroying the Somalian people.

This charitable effort, however, was hindered by Aideed. He and
his troops, in terroristic fashion, made sure none of the country's

citizens could get access to the food and supplies donated by the U.N. It's estimated that more than 80 percent of the food brought in by international relief organizations was confiscated by Aideed's gang.

In 1992 the United States made a decision to step in. Then-President George Bush, in one of his last acts in the White House, formed Operation Restore Hope sending U.S. troops to lead the international intervention force. The objective of this 25,000-troop mission was to secure the trade routes in Somalia so food could get through to the people.

You may remember images of Marines landing on the beach at night while reporters waited there with their cameras and microphones to ask, "How does it feel to be here in Somalia?" Some young jarhead, looking confused because he's trying to stay tactical as CNN shines a spotlight in his face, proudly answered, "It feels good to be here helping the starving people of Africa."

"The world is a fine place and worth fighting for." (Ernest Hemingway)

Many of us saw the heart-breaking images on TV of starving kids with vultures lurking nearby and heard the reports of massive widespread death. Something needed to be done. Being the charitable nation we are, we sent in the U.S. Marines. Good. Way to go, USA. We'll have that place fixed up in no time. And indeed, within a year as it would seem from the news, we had the situation under control and we were already bringing the bulk of our troops home. Mission accomplished. Operation Restore Hope was a success. And that was pretty much what the American people knew about Somalia.

THE POSSE ★ 21

Here was the reality. In a starving country devoid of hope, food meant power. Control the food; control the power. Damn anyone who might be convoying those shipments in the name of world peace. Say, for instance, the twenty-two Pakistani U.N. peacekeepers who were blown to kingdom come and gunned down by Aideed's men. When American troops were assigned to guard the food shipments, Aideed began to attack the U.S. When Marines and other U.S. soldiers started dying as a result of this third-world thug, it was time to "do something." That something was called Task Force Ranger (TFR).

Approved by the brand new Clinton administration, TFR was a top secret, joint military special operations package consisting of Army Special Forces, Delta operators, Rangers, Night Stalkers of the 160th Special Operations Air Regiment, Navy SEALs, and Air Force commandos. We were an unprecedented assault force brought together for one primary objective—hunt down and capture an enemy of the United States. The mission was named Gothic Serpent. The cover story was that we were there to support UNISOM (United Nations Operations in Somalia). The truth was, we were tasked to find and capture a warlord. If we couldn't get him, we'd start targeting his infrastructure.

We were not part of the humanitarian mission to feed the starving people of Somalia nor were we there to keep the peace. Rangers wouldn't know how to do that anyway. We came to kick in doors and shoot any bad guys who tried to resist. We were a military posse of America's elite sent on a man-hunt in the streets of the African Wild West.

"People sleep peaceably in their beds
at night only because rough men stand ready
to do violence on their behalf."
(Attributed to George Orwell)

We were one company of Rangers (Bco) from the 3rd Ranger Battalion of the 75th Ranger Regiment in Fort Benning, Georgia. Rangers are a highly trained, highly motivated infantry unit, storm troopers, really, who specialize in raids and dangerous missions behind enemy lines. We were, for the most part, young soldiers on our first enlistment, held to an incredibly high standard. We lived and breathed the six stanzas of the Ranger Creed that could be summed up in the Ranger motto "Rangers lead the way!"

Though they tried to blend in, the most covert and arguably most noticeable asset to TFR was the one squadron of Delta Force soldiers from Fort Bragg, North Carolina. They cut their hair down to the high and tight standards of the young Rangers to try and look a bit more inconspicuous. But it's hard to hide a bunch of men who physically resembled superheroes, long hair or not. Delta Force are your NFL pro-bowl players, the NBA all-stars of Army special operations. We called them the "varsity squad" and "big brother" because they were who we, as young Rangers, wanted to be and most looked up to.

Seasoned commandos with years of experience in the special operations community, Delta operators are trained to do just about anything you can imagine. In fact, sometimes their missions are so top-secret the Army doesn't acknowledge their existence. But trust me, they are very real. Keep that in mind the next time you happen to read a story in USA Today's world news section that says something like "Coalition Forces Apprehend Top Taliban Terrorist." The article will tell you how the Iraqi police are showing great improvement and making tremendous strides in their efforts to stand on their own. In fact, they have far surpassed expectations by having, all by themselves, captured two of the top most-wanted al-Qaeda in all of Iraq. Sure, they did it by themselves. Special operators never ask for credit. They just get the job done.

The air asset of TFR belonged to the 160th Special Operations Air Regiment out of Fort Campbell, Kentucky. These guys were my heroes. In the many years I got to work with them, I never once saw them even put on a landing light. The Night Stalkers are the Army's elite helicopter unit. They are the Captain Kirks of Army aviation—incredible pilots and crews absolutely dependable in their ability to transport and support the men on the ground in any type of weather, terrain, or combat situation, be it day or preferably night. "Night Stalkers Don't Quit!"

In addition to the Army's elite, we also had other services added to the mix for the benefit of their unique skill set. There was a team of high-speed sailors who had tattoos of small-flippered sea mammals on their arms. The Navy doesn't like to talk about what they do either, but they were there.

Of course, the government wanted its stake in the game so there were various three-letter spooky agency people dispersed among us who never seemed to have had any sort of identification except for a first name. "GI Jane" was one of the operatives we nicknamed. Funny when you are surrounded by nothing but men for months at a time, a woman within the ranks starts to take on supermodel looks and Wonder Woman capabilities. At least that's how I like to remember her.

The Air Force lent us their best with a small contingent of combat controllers (CCT) and pararescue guys (PJ). CCT are Air Force ground troops who specialize in pathfinder, air traffic control, and fire-support type operations. They are often assigned individually or as a team to other special operations forces like Special Forces or Navy SEAL teams to help provide expert air coordination and communications capabilities. PJs are basically warrior medics, trained to go in behind enemy lines to get a downed pilot or crew member, keep them alive, and, if need be, fight to carry them home.

You know I never did get to hang out much with the Air Force guys. I think they may have been at the beach in their condominiums the Air Force flew in for them. Yeah, I was pretty sure they were having BBQs and hanging out with the Swedish nurses from the U.N. compound. There is an amazing benefit to working for the Air Force, which is usually lacking in the Army. It's called "quality of life." Whereas the Army is singularly focused on accomplishing the mission first, the Air Force has a very unique way of doing business—let's take care of our people first and then we'll see about getting the job done.

The Air Force is a good gig, especially if you make it into the special operations side of it. You get to train hard at a high-speed, cool-guy job, and you have the best accommodations the military can afford. I think I would have liked working in the Air Force alongside the PJs and CCT guys. They all seemed to love their jobs, were incredibly smart, and had a much more fun and laid-back attitude than the strict discipline of the Ranger Regiment.

I get the chance to speak to a lot of high school students. Usually an Army recruiter will show up and make his presence known just in case the kids have any questions about a career in the Army. I think my military service and the fact I'm now a full-time working musician is good ammunition for a recruiter burdened with the monumental task of meeting the Army's quotas.

He can say something like, "Look kids. You can serve honorably in the Army and still be able to get out and do anything you want. Look at Keni. He's a famous country music star and he even has long hair!"

Inevitably some kid is going to come up to me after my speech and, in an enthusiastic voice, tell me of his immediate plans for the future. "Hey Keni, I'm thinking of joining the Army. You got any advice?"

I'll look around to make sure the Army recruiter is out of earshot. Then I'll lean into the young man and give him a covert answer as if I'm a spy unloading the best-kept secret that no Army, Navy, or Marine recruiter would ever dare tell you. "Yes. Here's my advice. Join the Air Force! It's about quality of life."

"Aim High" (the Air Force Recruiting Motto)

The different units of Task Force Ranger were broken down into its own divisions of squads and teams and job responsibility. The military is very good at breaking down big groups of people into smaller, more manageable sub-groups of people. For instance, the 75th Ranger Regiment is made up of four battalions.

Ours was the 3rd Battalion and there were four companies within the battalion: Aco, Bco (ours), Cco, and HQ. Each company consists of about 150 men organized into four platoons. Each platoon is divided into four squads. Each squad is split into two teams. In most infantry units, a squad is about eight to ten men. The Rangers have always been a little short handed. So my squad only had five men. I'd like you to meet them.

There was Doug Boren, my buddy from Texas. He was the squad leader. Typically, there are two team leaders under the squad leader, but since we didn't have enough guys, we only had one team leader— me. Doug and I were the same rank, first-time noncommissioned officers or E-5 buck sergeants. Since Doug had been in the Army longer than me by like a minute and a half, he officially outranked me.

I asked my platoon sergeant, SFC Sean T. Watson about that once. "How come Sgt. Boren gets to be the squad leader and I don't?"

"Because he's from Texas!"

You know, I still haven't figured that one out. Apparently Texas outranks the rest of the nation.

Doug and I worked well together. We became good friends and most of the time, he was pretty laid-back. To me, Doug was a great example of the "quiet professional" we were all supposed to be. He didn't yell much. Didn't really have to. The example he set did most of the talking.

Physically, Doug was a stud. In fact, a few years later he would go on to achieve a second place finish in the world renowned Best Ranger Competition. This event happens once a year at the Ranger training camp in Fort Benning. Units from all around the globe send their best to compete in an incredibly grueling and physically exhausting three-day event where two-man buddy teams are pushed to their physical and mental limit. Can you imagine what it was like being in a squad with a world-class athlete and trying to keep up with him on a daily basis? Doug set the standard for others to follow. And he set the standard high.

Specialist Melvin Dejesus had his "tab," meaning he successfully graduated from Ranger School and earned the right to dawn the coveted RANGER tab on his left shoulder above the 3rd Ranger Battalion scroll. For any Ranger serving in the 75th Ranger Regiment, "the tab" is a right of passage. If you are going to advance in the Rangers, you have to have your tab. Earn your tab, enjoy a new level of respect among your peers.

Any man can enlist in the Ranger Regiment. Not every man can stay. And even fewer last long enough for us to send them to Ranger School. It usually takes about a year toughing it out as a private before you get sent to the school. And that only happens when your squad leader feels you have demonstrated the mental and physical fortitude required to successfully complete the course. Most of the military sends soldiers with years of rank and experience. The Ranger Regiment sends privates. But we don't send people to fail. We offer a pre-Ranger course privates go through just to make sure they are ready for the real deal.

Ranger School is not a part of the 75th Ranger Regiment. It is the Army's premier leadership school and is open to all services. It's an intense and difficult course where you learn how to lead men in small-unit tactics under the most stressful combat situations a training course can re-create. Only a handful of those who start Ranger School actually finish and graduate. It is sixty-one days long and takes place in three different training environments.

There used to be a fourth phase that was held in the desert. Ironically the desert phase is no longer a part of Ranger School. Seems rather short-sighted they would cancel it back in 1995 given that less than a decade later, we would be fighting a war in deserts on two fronts. Maybe I'm just jealous because when I went through the school (back when it was hard), I had to endure two weeks in the desert in Fort Bliss, Texas. Don't let the name fool you. I still have the cracks in my fingers where the heat of the sun turned my skin into alligator hide. Desert phase or not, anyone who completes Ranger School has truly earned the right to wear that tab.

Somewhere along the way, Dejesus picked up the name "the Roach." I couldn't tell you how half the guys got their nicknames, but if it sounded funny and was fun to say, it stuck. Now that he was back from Ranger School, the Roach was promoted to the rank of Specialist pay grade E-4, and it was time to groom him into becoming a new team leader. Stereotypically, a young Ranger with a brand new tab is legend to be a fire-breathing, smack-talking stud who strikes fear into his enemies and his subordinates.

Generally this is true since the young soldiers are eager to dish out a little of what they have been taking for the past year. But I think

Dejesus was influenced in a good way by the laid-back leadership style Doug and I enacted. Dejesus was more mature than most. He had a pretty level head and, like us, never felt the need to do a lot of yelling. I was glad for it because that was not usually the case with other new E-4s.

Dejesus was like a lot of guys who find their way into the Rangers. He was a hard young man, an overachiever looking for something challenging that would turn him into his definition of what a man should be. Melvin grew up in Puerto Rico. Didn't have the best relationship with his father. Probably joined the Army because the judge gave him the option.

"Mr. Dejesus. You can join the Army, or you can go to jail. What is it going to be, son?"

"I'll take the Army!"

You know the kind. Because he was such a tough guy, you couldn't throw anything at the Roach he hadn't already seen back in the hood. At least that's what he would jokingly tell you. It went something like this,

"Men, this is a Carl Gustav rocket launcher. It can penetrate six inches of armored steel. Any questions?"

"Yes, Specialist Dejesus?"

"Yo man, in Puerto Rico, everyone had a rocket launcher!"

Let me put it this way. I was glad Dejesus was on our side and even happier to have him on my team.

There was Private First Class Eric Suranski who came from the Midwest. He was a good solid guy who, for the most part, was squared away. I liked having him. He did what he was told and did it well. As a team leader, that's the most you could ask from someone under your charge.

Whereas Dejesus was a tough guy, Eric was a thinker. He completed a couple years of community college and wanted to serve his country for a while, so he joined the Army. He wanted to be challenged, so he enlisted for a shot at the Rangers. I say "a shot at" because that's all an enlistment contract to the 75th Ranger Regiment will get you.

You can ask a recruiter for your choice of duty station, and the response is always the same. The recruiter will tell you all kinds of lies about how he doesn't have that many slots available and how he once wanted to be in the Ranger Regiment himself. But while he was serving as a "Marine-recon-Navy-Ranger-SEAL," he came down with a rare case of the "kneezles" and "cronic toelio" so he physically just couldn't do it anymore. And that's why he's stuck behind a desk now.

I can hear that recruiter even now. "Besides, what do you want to be a Ranger for anyway? Rangers are crazy. Jumping out of planes, eating snakes, and that kind of thing. What if you wash out? Then what? You'll get booted out and sent Army-wide with no options in accordance with the Army's needs. Wouldn't you rather go into communications? I can guarantee you a commo school slot right now. That way you'll have a life skill to fall back on once you're out of the Army. Oh son! And if you sign right here today, I can guarantee you money for college and we'll even pay off your student loans!"

But guys like Eric Suranski, Melvin Dejesus, and Doug Boren don't join up for the college money. They don't join up to learn a skill set to "fall back on in the real world." And they certainly don't worry about washing out because they don't see themselves as capable of failing. Guarantees can only take you so far. The rest is contingent upon your ability to meet or surpass the challenges and requirements set before you. Which brings me to Floyd.

David Floyd was from somewhere in South "Cackalacky" Carolina. When I first met him, he seemed to me to be what we in the South politely call a "bless your heart" kind of fellow. Meaning, you see him coming and the only polite response you can think of is "Oh man, bless your heart." Physically he was a spitting image of Barney Fife. Weighed about 130 pounds on a wet day. He was good-natured and kind-hearted. But when he first got to us, he was like many of us were in the beginning, "soup." Soup is short for soup sandwich. Which, as you can imagine, is about as useful as a screen door on a submarine.

I don't want to sell Floyd short as a soldier, because he did make it into the Ranger Regiment which is not an easy place to get to. There's a lengthy process of weeding out that takes place long before you ever set foot into a Ranger Battalion. You have to get through basic training, then Advanced Individual Training or AIT. If you graduate both programs and you are on a path to the Ranger Regiment, you then head straight to Airborne School.

Upon graduating Airborne School, and I mean within an hour of the graduation ceremony, you are marched down the road to RASP (Ranger Assessment and Selection Process). This is a two-month long Ranger indoctrination course designed to assess your physical and mental toughness as well as get you up to speed with regimental standard operating procedures. Remember the Rangers are deployable 24/7. With regular combat rotations already in place to Iraq and Afghanistan, it's highly likely a Ranger recruit, brand new to the Regiment, can find himself arriving and deploying within the same month. The rigorous demands of RASP are put in place to ensure the new Ranger has the skill set necessary to hit the ground running and be an asset to himself and his squad.

The 75th Ranger Regiment is the premier light-infantry unit in the Army. Their mission is to "plan and conduct special missions in support of U.S. policy and objectives." They are the absolute best at what they do. You can only be the best if you work with and hire the best people. As far as the Rangers, that was the point of making it so hard to get in. We were expected to be the best. So we only wanted the best.

How Floyd made it through all those courses and into the 3rd Ranger Battalion was a miracle and, if anything, a testament to his mental fortitude. Because I'm telling you, it seemed like that young man couldn't get anything right the first time.

The Army sets standards. The Rangers set those standards just a little higher. There are physical fitness standards, proficiency standards, even written standards. As the guy in charge of him, Floyd was a pain in my butt because it meant extra work seeing as how he was constantly in need of "retraining."

For instance, once a quarter we would do a road march for proficiency sake. It's a twelve-mile walk where you carry fifty pounds on your back and have only three hours to do it. Most people can walk a mile every fifteen minutes. Do it wearing combat boots, dressed in full gear with a 50-lb rucksack on your back, and though it's still doable, it doesn't feel good. Your shoulders ache. Your feet have blisters. You are tired. Usually the marches are strategically scheduled right before the weekend, so at least you have a two-day break afterward.

I once made the mistake of letting Floyd fall back. I wanted to show everyone how fast I was and I sure wasn't gonna let this newbie slow me down and make me look bad. The problem was, if Floyd came in just a minute late, then he failed to meet the standard. And who do you think got yelled at for that one?

"Sergeant Thomas! Get in here! Why didn't Floyd pass his road march? Why didn't he meet the standard? What is wrong with you?"

What is wrong with me? Sergeant Watson cared very little how fast I was, how hard I was, or that Doug and I scared the newbies with our speed. What he cared about was that everyone in his platoon met the standard.

So come Saturday morning when everyone else was enjoying their weekend off, who was out in the field with aching shoulders and blistered toes walking that twelve-mile road march AGAIN? You are correct. David Floyd. But so was Doug Boren, Keni Thomas, Melvin Dejesus, and Eric Suranski. You may think "Well, that's not fair. Floyd screwed up. He should take responsibility for his own actions and push himself to pass what he failed to accomplish." True. He should take responsibility for his own action. But SFC Watson was trying to teach me what I as a young leader had yet to learn.

You are only as good as your weakest link. So it wasn't just Floyd who failed. We had failed Floyd because we left him behind.

"A house divided against itself will not stand."
(Matthew 12:25 NKJV)

When someone on our team, staff or unit doesn't pull their weight, we have a tendency to distance ourselves from that person. We think, "I'm better than they are. I don't want to be associated with a loser. Can't be slowed down. Gotta move forward. Gotta show everyone how good I am. I can't worry about someone else. I've got problems of my own."

We take on a "survival of the fittest" mentality and leave the other person behind in order to save ourselves. By allowing someone else to fail, we somehow reason that by setting ourselves apart from them, it makes us look better, because we have met the standard, accomplished the goal, or surpassed expectations while others could not. But as a person who leads by example, it's the wrong answer. I understand it is never an easy thing to pull someone aside and say, "Hey, you're not holding up your end. You seem to be having a hard time carrying your load. We need you to get up to speed because the team can't function without you. How can I help?"

I know how tough that conversation is to have. It certainly would be easier to just avoid it, let the person fail, and maybe they'll get fired or fade away. You know why it's such a difficult thing to do? Because it's going to take extra effort on your part. As a person who strives to set an example for others to follow, the burden of leadership is on your shoulders.

Peter understood well the importance of leading by example. He made it a point to remind Christians that they are being looked at, to set an example for others to follow even when there is no immediate or perceivable self-gain.

"Shepherd the flock of God which is among you, serving as overseers, not by compulsion but willingly, not for dishonest gain but eagerly; nor as being lords over those entrusted to you, but being examples to the flock." (1 Peter 5:2–3 NKJV)

I don't think Peter was talking only to the folks in charge who we might typically think are the "lords over us." He was making a point that we are all leaders by the example we set. Unless we happen to be the Grand Poobah, we seldom get to choose who we work with. But we do get to choose who we work for. When you took on that job, accepted that position, joined that church, volunteered your time to that cause, you raised your right hand and said, "Give me the job. You can count on me. Send me."

You have then become part of something much larger than yourself. You have become part of what is called a team where there is always a person to your left and to your right. And those people are counting on you. Begin to see yourself as important, and you will begin to live up to it. That means doing the hard work even when it doesn't necessarily mean you will be patted on the back for it. The gain is in the greatness of your team.

You may not get to choose the people you work with. But what you can do is hold them to a higher standard. Set your standards high and bring your team up to meet those standards.

If you bring your standards down to accommodate everyone, then what do you have? You have mediocrity. And nobody wants to be part of an average team. We want to be winners. We want to be great. We want to know at the end of the day our part was one that contributed to greatness and excellence.

You've never heard a coach in a press conference on Saturday or Sunday afternoon come on TV, look the camera in the eye, and say, "I think we're looking pretty mediocre, everyone feels good about themselves. This is gonna be great. We're gonna go out there and do our best."

That would be ridiculous. Champions talk about working hard, being prepared, and giving every ounce of effort they have so they know, win or lose, they left everything on the field. You train as you fight so you will fight as you train. You will only be as good as you prepared yourself to be. Your team will only be as good as the sum of its parts. If you are going to be counted on as the Army's premiere light infantry special operations unit, then you better make certain everyone is up to the task.

"Now the body is not made up of one part
but of many." (1 Corinthians 12:14)

Floyd was our machine gunner. If he wasn't up to speed on that weapon system, if he couldn't handle it like an absolute expert, then we couldn't count on him. If the gun goes down, the squad is in trouble. If the squad falters, the platoon is crippled. Once that happens, the mission is lost. David Floyd was the one piece of the puzzle that made everything work. The many lives and millions of dollars spent to send TFR into Somalia all hinged on David Floyd and his ability to do his job while setting an example for others to follow.

Begin to see yourself as important and you will begin to live up to it.

So push, pull, or drag, we made sure Floyd got across that finish line and met the high standard we set for ourselves. We needed Floyd. We couldn't afford to just get rid of him and let him fall behind. Because as good as I am, I cannot do it all. And guess what? Neither can you.

"You're going to wear yourself out—
and the people, too. This job is too heavy
a burden for you to handle all by yourself."
(Exodus 18:18 NLT)

My squad in front of the Gunslinger. Me, Spc. Melvin Dejesus, Private David Floyd, Sgt. Doug Boren, Private Pete Neathery, and Private Eric Suranski.

Chapter 3

TRAIN AS YOU FIGHT. FIGHT AS YOU TRAIN.

Energetically will I meet the enemies of my country.
I shall defeat them on the field of battle for I am
better trained and will fight with all my might.
—5TH STANZA OF THE RANGER CREED

ALL AROUND THE AIRPLANE HANGAR you could hear the clanging of weapons as men geared up—loading down their bodies with heavy Kevlar bulletproof plates, radios, ammunition, grenades, smoke canisters, flash bangs, and other crowd dispersal devices. I remember looking over at the Delta guys and, even after all these weeks of working with them, still being impressed by their calm seriousness and especially by all their high-speed modified weapon systems.

Like Ironman dawning his futuristic armor, these men looked every bit the part of a warrior superhero.

For the most part, our Rangers were less experienced than the "Varsity Squad," so there was a lot of gibber jabber and posturing going on among the young men. Nervousness was camouflaged with joking and bravado in an attempt to squash the stress that was beginning to build. What do you think is going on in the mind of a young man like Floyd who's been in the Army all of about three and half minutes? He's thinking, *Man if this thing goes down for real, I hope I don't screw up. I don't want to let my buddies down.*

The seasoned pros, however, don't have to worry about screwing up. They don't even think about it. It's not an option. Why? They know their job. They know they are prepared. They know they are ready. They know exactly what is expected of them because they have done the hard work repeatedly for years in advance. So instead of stressing, they spend their prep time thinking through the mission and the specific tasks before them.

As I was going down the line doing my double checks with my guys, Doug and Sergeant First Class Watson were returning from the briefing room with the warning order. This is a fancy way of saying the mission-brief. Sergeant Watson walked out with an 8 x 10 photograph of our objective and laid it on the ground in the middle of the platoon right next to our bunks.

"All right, everybody gather around."

We huddled up and looked down at a black and white aerial view of downtown Mogadishu taken from about 200 feet up. There was a building near the corner of a main intersection circled in red ink.

"This is the target building. And this is the corner of the building we are roping in at. Any questions?"

That was about it. Ten minutes ago I was in shorts and flip-flops, writing a letter home and enjoying a day off. Wasn't even supposed to be working. Then, in less time than it takes for most of us to even show up to a meeting, Task Force Ranger was roaring to life in full operational mode.

We had our mission. We had our plan. We knew who we were after, where we were going, how we would get there, how we would get out, and had a backup plan to that. We were fully armed, locked and loaded, headed out to the aircraft with rotors spinning in a mental mind-set ready for combat.

Do not mistake that minimal time spent in the huddle with being poorly prepared. This was no last-second-sandlot-hail-mary-game-winning idea we scribbled in the sand. No sir. A championship franchise does not wing it. Any good coach of any great team will tell you victory is dependent on prior preparation. Proper planning is essential. Imagine any scenario. "What if" it to death. Come up with a solid, feasible contingency plan for all the possible situations your mission might call for. Once you have a plan in place, you then implement tough, realistic training where you rehearse, practice, drill, adjust, and perfect your plan so every individual knows exactly what is expected of them and is as good as they possibly can be at their particular part of the job.

It takes more than just recruiting a bunch of top round draft picks, setting them loose on the field, and expecting them to perform at a championship level. You have to practice, and practice hard. It's not enough for a team to have great plays and spend their afternoons at practice simply running walkthroughs of the playbook.

It's like the young man who was visiting New York City and asked a lady carrying a violin case for directions. "Excuse me, ma'am," he said. "Can you tell me how to get to Carnegie Hall?" The lady answered, "Practice."

If you are going to be the best you can be, which is what your team expects of you, then you have to do the hard work in advance. You learn the plays. You run the drills. You do it repeatedly, time and time again, until every player knows exactly what is expected of them and can do so with perfection under any given circumstance.

That way, come game time, you know without a doubt the hard work has been done and you and your team are ready. Great leaders understand this. In fact, the very first SEAL team commander made his mantra, "If you are called upon to do anything and you are not ready, in that moment you have already failed."

Get ready by training. If you are a softball player and you want to improve your batting, you go to practice and take swings against your team's best pitchers. A soccer goalie gets pounded with shots by his own teammates every day. Football players hit each other hard in scrimmage. I had a friend in college who viewed swim practice as a test of her tolerance to pain. How far could she push herself every yard of that pool? Mary Wayte would go on to win four Olympic medals, including two golds.

Rangers have a saying "Train as you fight. Fight as you train." The Boy Scouts have it right too. Their motto is "Be prepared." Because when it comes down to it, you will only be as good as you prepared yourself to be. The people around you will only be as good as you trained them to be. So the idea is to make everyone an absolute expert at their job. This is your best chance to ensure the mission is successfully accomplished and everyone makes it back alive.

Each unit in TFR had their own level of expertise and their own standard operating procedures or SOPs. SOP is an official-sounding military acronym for "this is how we do it." If it gets done on a regular basis in the military, there's gonna be an SOP for it. This is how you carry a weapon. This is how you clear a room. This is how you rig an explosive. This is how you call for fire and talk to the aircraft. This is how you dress. This is how you walk, talk, roll your socks, and use the latrine.

Since each unit of Task Force Ranger had its own SOPs, obviously the challenge was getting everyone on the same page. So how do you bring 400 Type A personalities together so everyone works in cohesion despite their differences? You shoot together. You move together. You communicate as one. You train as you fight so you will fight as you have trained.

As a unit, we ran through all kinds of imaginable live-fire contingency plans and mission scenarios. Delta Force, Rangers, Air Force operators, snipers, SEALs, pilots and crew, air assets, ground vehicles—we all learned to work together seamlessly through constant hours of tough realistic training.

Here's where the assault force will go. Here's where the blocking force will go. Here's where the Reaction Force and the vehicles will route. What if we get to Aideed when he's in a building and attempts to run on foot? Here's what we will do. What if he's in a car? Here's what we will do. What if he's getting away on a camel? Here's what we will do. (Shoot the camel.)

We even rehearsed getting in and out of an aircraft in the most efficient manner possible. We found out early on, it takes a great deal of orchestration to pack a dozen men fully loaded with combat gear into the cargo bay of a Black Hawk helicopter and then get them out most expeditiously.

Best of all, each and every one of us became absolute masters of our weapons. We got to fire everything we had in our arsenal and did so repeatedly. Pistols. Machine guns. Grenade launchers.

Demolition. Claymores. Rocket launchers. We perfected our quick-fire techniques and became absolutely lethal with a rifle.

We fired so many rounds down range and spent so much time out in those sand dunes, that through repetition the basics became second nature. And that's exactly what you want. When a task becomes second nature, it means there's one less stress that has been relieved. One less thing young Suranski has to worry about. The basics of "shoot, move, and communicate" should be automatic to him. Because when people start shooting at him, he's going to be stressed enough. He certainly doesn't need to worry about trying to remember how to work his M203 grenade launcher, where he's supposed to go, or how to pick up a radio.

As a leader, when you train as you fight, your confidence level builds. When you're confident, those around you have confidence in you. And, in turn, their confidence becomes stronger. General Patton said the single most important characteristic of a good soldier is self-confidence. Instilling confidence is about building trust at many different levels. And trust is something that must be gained. It cannot be issued.

A good soldier has confidence in the chain of command. You have got to have faith that the people in charge are consistently making good decisions and acting in your best interest. This was important especially in our case because our lives were on the line.

A lot was made of the fact the Clinton administration and Defense Secretary Les Aspin did not provide us with all the necessary equipment requested by our commanders. But as the soldier on the ground, that didn't concern me because I knew General Garrison would not send us in to do a job if he wasn't absolutely positive we could accomplish the mission with the assets we did have available.

Sure, we could have used a Spectre gunship (or a battleship off the coast so we could have sunk the whole city). That eye in the sky would have been a valuable asset. They can obliterate a single person target with lethal precision from 10,000 feet in the air. There are times I know we could have used that firepower. But there was a limit on how much and what kind of equipment (and how many men) Task Force Ranger could take. Spectre would have required a whole lot more people in Mogadishu than our government was willing to send. That was part of the political parameters set.

It is unfortunate when politics intervene and meddle with the military's needs. But when has it not? Remember, we were supposed to be pulling out of Somalia. The administration was concerned about the appearance of a significant troop escalation right after we told the world we were successfully leaving. Bottom line? More troops and weapons would not have made the U.S. look very good.

As the person being sent, you rarely get to be a part of the decision-making process. Les Aspin wasn't going to come down to the Ranger Regiment and hold a town hall meeting asking my opinion. That's why it's so important to have confidence your leadership is making great decisions at every level. I believed in General Garrison. If he said we can do it, then by God, we can do it.

I also had confidence Sergeant Watson had our backs. If Rangers, Delta, SEALs, and PJs are all Type A personalities, then he was a double A. I remember once back at Fort Benning, he gave us a squad leader briefing while sitting on the toilet. "Squad leaders! Get in here!" I'm telling you, it takes a confident man to hold a meeting while sitting on the toilet.

Sergeant First Class Watson was also never afraid to voice his opinion if he saw something out of line. More than once I saw him light up our company commander Captain Steele. "Hey sir. That's all screwed up!" He had a way with words. Every time, though, Watson made sure whatever problem he saw was remedied. I believed in the man. I would have followed Sean Watson anywhere.

A good soldier has to have confidence in their equipment. If correctly used, implemented and cared for, proper equipment will save your life.

"Put on the full armor of God so that you can take your stand against the devil's schemes." (Ephesians 6:11)

When I got out of the Army, I worked as a counselor for an outdoor therapeutic organization for problematic youth. There were tough guys and bullies, outcasts and misfits, good kids and bad kids. As troubled as some of them were, they were still kids and grossly lacking in self-confidence. They did not see themselves as someone capable of leadership and had no clue what it meant to be counted on. If we were to help them become boys with strong teamwork and leadership skills, the first order of business was to boost their esteem and instill self-confidence.

One of my most favorite things to do with the new kids was to take them rappelling. I'd climb them up to a big cliff, ask for volunteers, strap them into a rope harness, and then hang them over the edge. (I found it interesting that, without fail, the big talkers were always the last to volunteer for this exercise.)

Once I got them in the harness and coaxed them out over the edge, the first thing I told them to do was to let go of the rope. Why? To show them they can trust their equipment. The harness is not going to break. Once they realize the rope is secure, they now can get on with the most difficult part of the task—convincing themselves that yes, they can do this.

You should have seen the Superman smiles on the kids' faces when they finally made their way down the sixty-foot cliff. For kids who were told by the system they are failures, this type of accomplishment is invaluable in elevating their self-confidence. They have learned to trust the gear, to trust the training, to trust the person on the other end of the rope and, most importantly they have developed confidence in themselves.

Like a manifesto for life, the Bible too has some suggested spiritual equipment you'll probably want to take with you to successfully accomplish your mission. If Jesus were to huddle you up and issue you a packing list, it might look something like this:

1. Body Armor of Righteousness: "He put on righteousness as his body armor." (Isa. 59:17 NLT)
2. Shield of Faith: "My God is my rock, in whom I find protection, He is my shield, the power that saves me." (2 Sam. 22:3 NLT)
3. Sword of the Spirit: "the sword of the Spirit, which is the word of God." (Eph. 6:17)
4. Helmet of Salvation: "Take the helmet of salvation." (Eph. 6:17)

God's equipment inventory can keep on going to include shoes, belts, breastplates, arrows, chariots, arks, and more.

As with the kids who learn to trust the rope to safely hold them, the pieces of God's armor you choose to employ are only as effective as your faith. The more you use it. The better you get with it. Suit up, gear up. Get it on.

"Wars may be fought with weapons. But they are won by men." (General George Patton)

Proper planning and realistic training will get you ready for the game, but leadership is going to win it. This means leadership at every level. Not just the people at the top like the coaching staff, the manager, the big boss. Not even Major General Garrison who ran the entire package.

Leadership is not a position. It is the example you set. That means everyone must lead—from General Garrison to Sergeant First Class Watson, all the way down to the last man on the totem pole, Private David Floyd, the only person he was leading was himself.

TFR was a little over 400 strong, the bulk of which was force support. Mechanics. Medics. Armorers. Cooks. Staff. Intel guys. Electricians. The list goes on and on. It takes about three support folks to send one fighting man into the battlefield. No matter how great you are with a weapon, you can't get where you need to be without help. And you can't get help if help doesn't show up.

If the mechanic doesn't show up to work, the aircraft doesn't fly. If the aircraft doesn't fly, troops can't get where they need to be. If troops don't get where they need to be, the mission is a failure. And a failed mission is the least that can happen when one person on the team does not perform up to standard.

Think about this. What if the mechanic *does* show up to work, but doesn't show up 100 percent? Say he decides not to stick with the SOPs in place. Say he gets complacent and skips a couple steps. "Oh, I checked that yesterday and it's good to go."

Here's what happens. The boys load the aircraft. The aircraft takes to the sky. The flight pattern calls for evasive maneuvering. The pilot has to bank hard. And then like an uninvited drunk stumbling in to your child's birthday party, Murphy shows up at the worst of times. The torque converter the mechanic assumed was "good to go" was not good to go. The transmission fails. The tail rotor goes out throwing the bird into an unrecoverable spin. Newton then takes over and in accordance with law, hurtles the mass of machinery to the earth. Impact is inevitable and non-survivable. All sixteen aboard are killed. Sixteen people, each with their own families and loved ones who will now live the rest of their lives robbed of a father, mother, brother, sister, or a friend. A completely preventable mechanical issue could have, would have, and should have been caught with the SOPs set in place. But the one piece of the puzzle that mattered the most, the mechanic, did not do his job correctly.

When you raise your hand and take the job, when you put on the uniform and show up to work, you do so 100 percent and then some. Good is never good enough when better is expected.

The truth is, it's easy to lose perspective on just how much we matter to those around us. Perhaps you think that in your job or your day-to-day routine, lives are not on the line. I say you are undervaluing the role you play on the team for which you have volunteered to be a part. You may not fly around in a Black Hawk helicopter and carry an M4 rifle on the field of battle. You might be a seventh grade teacher who uses the classroom to change a life. Maybe you volunteer your time to a passionate and worthy cause or a charitable program. And what if you are the office worker in your cubicle on the 60th floor of a big corporation giving your all to the task at hand?

Your presence matters. Those people on your left and right are directly affected by the result of your actions. Their success as a whole depends entirely on you because you are the one piece of the puzzle that makes everything come together. As a parent, volunteer, manager, consultant, teacher or a student, you have a job to do and a standard to uphold.

"Whatever your hand finds to do, do it with all your might." (Ecclesiastes 9:10)

We were told in retrospect TFR was outnumbered 10 to 1. In total, we lost 19 men and 78 were officially wounded while in Mogadishu. Somali casualties were well into the thousands. Our losses would have been significantly higher had it not been for our high level of planning, the intensity of our training, and the outstanding leadership at every level—from General Garrison who ran the entire package, with decades of experience, all the way down to young Private David Floyd, who was in charge of no one but himself.

When plans go awry, which they most certainly will do during the chaos of combat and life in general, training will take over and give you the advantage. But great leadership will ultimately save the day.

By the time that photo was slapped on the ground showing our objective, every single one of us already knew exactly what needed to happen and what was expected. It was time to get it on!

We left the hangar and headed for the birds, walking with a sense of purpose and forming ourselves into our chalks. For accountability purposes, each helicopter always carried the same group of passengers called a "chalk," which was usually about twelve men for the Black Hawks. I was on Chalk 3 with SFC Watson as the chalk leader. As we moved out across the tarmac, you could already hear the rotors winding up with that high-pitched whine of the MH-60 turbine engines.

I looked around and saw Delta operators adjusting their gear as they sat down on the bench seats attached to the skids of the Little

Birds. There were other Rangers scrambling up into the Humvees, gun Jeeps, and 5-ton trucks. I would see them soon at the objective since they were our ride out of there. We locked and loaded our weapons. I double-checked that the safety was on for both my rifle and the shotgun. As I waited for my squad to climb into our side of Super 66, I looked over at Chalk 4 as my best friend Casey was climbing aboard Super 67. It would be the last time I saw him.

Heading out into the sand dunes for daily training.

Chapter 4

ROPES

*Acknowledging the fact that a Ranger is a more elite soldier who
arrives at the cutting edge of battle by land, sea, or air.*
—2ND STANZA OF THE RANGER CREED

"IRENE!" THAT WAS THE CODE word for a mission go. The pilots
repeated it. Sergeant First Class Watson repeated it. We all repeated
it. This was no "signature flight." I thought, *This is for real. Here we go.*

The Black Hawk jerked just a bit as it broke free from the earth's
grip. It lifted and moved forward with a violent sense of purpose.
Super 66 screamed away from the airfield headed for a fight. She
was appropriately named *Gunslinger,* which was painted in black on
the engine above the cargo door. I always liked that name. This was
the Wild West and we were the law in town.

I was sitting on the rope in the left-side door. Just in front of me, with their knees in the breeze and their legs dangling over the Ivory Coast was Doug, Floyd, and Pete Neathery, an M60 machine gunner who was assigned to our squad. Suranski and the Roach were next to me. We were packed in on the left side. Another squad from our platoon was on the right. Sergeant First Class Watson was the chalk leader and sat in the middle facing us with his back to the pilots. He had a headset on and would relay the information being passed along over the radio.

At about three minutes out, we got a call saying bad guys were spotted on the objective with heavy weapon systems. We were going in hot!

The Black Hawk is a violent machine. It's loud. It shakes. It fights the pilot as the main rotors go one way and the tail rotor goes another. Whereas an airplane is designed to smoothly lift off the ground and wants to fly up and away, the UH-60 feels more like a maverick stallion beating the air into submission. With two mini-guns sticking out the windows, it's a mean looking machine. Skimming across the surface of the Indian Ocean, the awesome sight of those big black helicopters reaching the shoreline must have looked like a small armada of impending doom to the Somali militia, who were scattering into their positions and hastily preparing for our arrival.

The Delta and Ranger assault force was formidable, consisting of seventy-five Rangers and forty Delta soldiers who would be inserted by four MH-6 Little Birds and six MH-60 Black Hawks. There were also four AH-6J Little Bird gunships providing close air support. The ground convoy or Reaction Force was made up of about fifty men on a dozen vehicles that would rendezvous with us at the target building and provide our extraction.

This was a daring daylight raid into the heart of Mogadishu near an area of town called the Bakara Market where militia were known to gather, and small arms were known to be stockpiled. We called it Indian Country. On a Sunday afternoon it was also the busiest part of the city. Not the most ideal time and place for a raid. But we didn't get to choose where and when the bad guys decide to show up. According to our intel, a handful of Aideed's top people were still meeting in a building right across from the Olympic Hotel, an easily identifiable landmark. If we got there fast enough, we could catch them.

We made our approach along the outskirts of town where the houses turn to huts and huts give way to desert. In order to somewhat disguise our flight plan, we would fly just a little past our objective and then come back to it. Up ahead just off to our left, I could see another Black Hawk loaded with Rangers. I am certain they were thinking the same thing as I was, "Lord, make me the man You trained me to be." Super 66 began to bank hard-right back toward the target and forever into history.

It's clear what runs through your mind when the sense of urgency begins to tack into the red. Sure, there is nervousness. But it's not a scared-of-the-dark-or-haunted-house kind of nervous. To me, it was exactly like what an athlete feels in the starting block just before the gun goes off. He is going through each step of the race in his mind— start to finish, hurdle by hurdle, stroke by stroke. Picture it. Mentally prepare. Focus. Mentally prepare. See it. Mentally prepare.

I ran through the mission in my head. What are my immediate responsibilities as a team leader in the door of the aircraft? What are my responsibilities once I hit the ground?

"One minute!"

We came in from the north at about sixty feet off the ground and split into two lines of approaching flights. Super 66 stayed over Hawlwadig Road, one of the only paved main roads in the city. Across from me, a block over to the east, I could see the other Black Hawks slow down and begin creeping above the street just like we were doing. I could see the Rangers sitting in the door, staring into the dust, and anxiously waiting for the one word—"ropes"—that would get them out of that aircraft and onto the ground where they felt most at home. But we don't kick the ropes until we are over the target.

The plan was a basic template insertion. Delta would come in on Little Birds and hit the building first. The MH-6 Little Bird is a two-man gunship with a bubbled cockpit that can maneuver just about anywhere space allows. Those pilots could land on a roof, at a door, on a car, in a box, in a tree with a fox, here or there, these guys could land anywhere. The operators would sit in the open air on benches fastened to the skids. When the skids touched down, all they had to do was literally step off and begin storming the building and clearing rooms.

Little Birds would come in first. Then the Rangers would follow immediately behind on the Black Hawks. We would rope in at all four corners of the building and secure a perimeter around the building. The assault guys were free to do their jobs on the inside knowing we had their backs on the outside.

As a team leader in the door of the aircraft, I had two tasks while in the air. The first of which was to "confirm the target building and confer with the crew chief." As we made our approach, I leaned out the door, looking ahead to try and spot the objective. Doug told me to "move," because he couldn't see our crew chief Staff Sergeant Hargis, who was supposed to give us the word to throw out the ropes. I don't know why Doug was so worried about what Hargis was looking at, because neither Doug nor I could have told you where the target building was. None of us could see a thing.

The pilots called it "brown out." There was so much dust being kicked up by the rotors that it was practically impossible to see anything. Dirt was swirling around in the cockpit and I don't know how the pilots could tell where they were going. I thought, *Well, maybe the Black Hawk has some sort of special "dust-buster" radar equipment.* In reality, the *Gunslinger* had little more than windshield wipers and the skill of the pilots to guide us through that storm.

Every few seconds or so, you would catch a glimpse of a rooftop. Now I'm not sure how many aerial photographs of third-world cities you've looked at, but I'm here to tell you rooftops around the world look pretty much the same. *No problem.* I'm thinking all I have to do is look for the building circled in red ink! No such luck. I couldn't have told you the difference between the Olympic Hotel and a Motel 6. We crossed over an intersection just like what I thought I remembered from the picture. I looked at Hargis, who was pointing at some power lines we were told to watch out for. I was certain we were over the target, so I told SFC Watson this was our intersection. He thought so too, but the helicopter kept creeping up the street. Obviously, we were both wrong.

Fortunately by design, my inept ability to "confirm the target" was not the only deciding contingency. Remember, we had the best pilots in the world. I never, not once, doubted those two men. I had complete confidence in their ability to put us exactly where we needed to be at exactly when we needed to be there every single time.

Chief Warrant Officer Stan Wood and I were not pals or best friends. We didn't hang out together talking about home and showing each other pictures of our wives and girlfriends. Chief Warrant Officer Gary Fuller didn't risk his neck and give an extra-special effort because he liked me. Those two pilots always came through for us, time and time again, because that was their job and they knew we were counting on them.

Chief Wood and Chief Fuller understood they were the one piece of the puzzle that made everything work. The lives of everyone on that mission, not to mention the millions of dollars spent on sending TFR into Somalia, all sat entirely upon their shoulders and their ability to do their job and do it precisely to standard.

Begin to see yourself as important and you will live up to it.

"Night Stalkers Don't Quit." (motto of the 160th Special Operations Air Regiment)

When you apply to the 160th as a pilot, you can only get there as a seasoned pro with hundreds of flight hours logged at other units. If accepted, you then have to move to a place like Fort Campbell, Kentucky, and every bit of your existence becomes immersed in the Night Stalker way of life. You train constantly. You are deployed more than 200 days a year. If you are a Black Hawk pilot, every working moment is all for one purpose and one purpose only. In fact, the Night Stalkers make it very clear what your entire mission is based upon. When you walk into the 160th for the first time, it's right there on the wall for you to see.

"Put the customer on target, on time, plus or minus thirty seconds."

Thirty seconds. That's the standard. Can you imagine if you tried to hold yourself to a thirty-second margin of error? Or worse yet, what if your boss did?

"You're late! You were supposed to be here at 8:30!"

"But it *is* 8:30, Mr. Boss Man."

"Nope. It's thirty seconds past. You're late. Don't do it again or you're fired."

To most of us, thirty seconds may seem a ridiculously unfair expectation. We would be constantly falling short. But not the Night Stalkers. On target. On time. Damn the dirt and dust.

When I was going through the Special Forces Combat Divers Course down in Key West, Florida, you were expected to accomplish numerous underwater navigational swims at night. You and your dive buddy would be dropped in a mile from shore in the dark. You were given a certain spot on the beach you were supposed to swim to, a compass to guide you, and a time frame in which to complete the mission.

One particular night, the current was very strong. My buddy John and I were fighting it the entire way in. It felt like we were swimming upstream. I could feel us drifting, but we weren't allowed to surface and eyeball the shore as a reference. So by the time we did hit the shallows and came up on the beach, we found ourselves way off target. In fact, most of the entire class of students landed off target. As tired as we were, we would all have to get back in the water and swim it again. The instructors knew exactly what they were doing. When students began complaining and blaming the unfair conditions in which we had to perform, the cadre fired back a one-liner that stuck.

"The tides and currents do not affect the combat diver. Shut up and dive."

The second time around though, everyone passed the swim because we now knew we had to adjust for the outgoing tides. The lesson that night was not about using a compass underwater in the dark. It was to teach us that factors beyond our control will inevitably arise making an already difficult task that much harder to accomplish. Blaming and crying doesn't change the outcome. It may be unfair, but never the less, the mission must be accomplished. As our brothers in the Marines will tell you: improvise, adapt, and overcome.

"Do what you can, with what you have, where
you are." (Theodore Roosevelt)

When the refugees of Israel were running from Egypt en route to
their new home far far away in Canaan, their escape and evasion plan
called for them to cross a desert. Their compass was a big ball of glowing dust that God had put out front to guide them to their target. As
the excitement of being free from oppression wore off and the reality
of life in the badlands kicked in, there was a lot of griping and grumbling. A short while into the trek they ran out of water. As the man in
charge, Moses got an earful.

> "So the people grumbled against Moses, saying, What are
> we to drink?" (Exod. 15:24)

Had it been me I would have lost it right there. "Look people,
three days ago you were dancing in gratitude because God drowned
the entire Egyptian Army in the Red Sea. Now you're already doubt-
ing Him? What a bunch of weenies. Everyone's fired!"

Fortunately for the Israelites, Moses had better leadership skills
than I would have had in that situation. He went to the higher-up and
found a solution. With God's help Moses made a temporary adjust-
ment to the situation by throwing a tree in some bitter water that
made it drinkable. It was just enough to keep the people moving forward. Moses then reiterated an order to his army of followers. He told
them to quit whining, listen to God "pay attention to his commands
and keep all his decrees" (Exod. 15:26), and move out.

And what do you know? Sure enough, soon after sucking it up
and driving on, the seemingly impossible became possible. "They

came to Elim, where there were twelve springs and seventy palm trees, and they camped there near the water" (Exod. 15:27).

Moses wasn't a Special Forces combat diver instructor. But had he been, I bet I know exactly what he would have said to motivate those sniveling, grumbling, belly-aching doubters and get them to accomplish the task at hand.

"The tides and currents do not affect the combat diver. Now shut up and dive!"

"It is not the strongest of the species that survives, nor the most intelligent that survives. It is the one that is the most adaptable to change. (Charles Darwin)

"Thirty seconds!" yelled Staff Sergeant Hargis. He was the crew chief on my side.

I couldn't really hear him over the rotors, but I didn't need to. We all knew the time was at hand because the bird began to flare. That's when I finally saw the target building. I could see the other Black Hawks come to a hover a block over. I could see Little Birds touching down as Delta operators stepped off and stormed the building. I could see them throwing people to the ground. And I could hear the gunfire begin. Here we go.

"Ropes!"

My next job was to shove the ninety feet of coiled three-inch thick rope we were sitting on out the door and make sure the end of it hits the ground. Seems simple enough. But I have to stress just how important it is to watch where the end of the rope lands. What if it lands in a pit of snakes? Obviously you don't want to go there. Or, as in the case of Chalk 4 behind us, the rope is hanging over something you can't slide down onto, a parked car. Their pilot had to drag the rope to an open area putting them about one hundred meters short of the target. Since the point of fast-roping is speed and efficiency, you want to be able to control your rate of descent and still hit the ground running. At night or in cases like this of limited visibility, anxious Rangers eager to exit an aircraft have been known to kick the rope and follow it out the door only to find they had run out of rope, impacting the earth like Wile E. Coyote.

This is simple math really. If the rope is only ninety feet long and the bird happens to be a hundred feet off the ground, it doesn't make for a good landing when you are coming down it like a runaway pile driver. Negative ten feet is ten feet too short. Not good.

Ropes go out both sides of the bird. Both ropes hit the ground.

"Go! Go! Go!"

Getting fifteen combat loaded men quickly out of a cargo area no bigger than an Escalade is somewhat of an orchestration, a very well-rehearsed orchestration. While hovering at a standstill just sixty feet off the ground, in the middle of a hostile city where everyone wants to shoot you, that big ole flying SUV and everyone inside becomes a vulnerable target. This would not be the time to begin figuring out who moves when and in what order. Plan and rehearse in advance to get your cargo out most expeditiously and get the bird back on its way riki tik.

Like Batman disappearing out of frame down the bat pole, I watched as my squad members zipped away one after the other and vanished into the cloud of brown. Gravity will gladly assist you out of any aircraft especially when you are weighted down with sixty-plus pounds of gear. Since you aren't harnessed or safe-tied in, it's very important to have a positive grip on the nylon braided rope before you commit.

In fact, one of the guys in Chalk 4 behind us, Private Todd Blackburn, lost his grip and plummeted sixty something feet to the ground, landing with a sickening thud. He broke his back, was knocked unconscious and out of the fight before it got started. Fortunately for young Private Blackburn, the Ranger medic Doc Marcus Good was right there to provide immediate care as was Sgt. First Class Bart Bullock the Delta medic. Since we had planned and trained for a casualty on infill, the process of safely evacuating Blackburn was well executed. He would live to tell about it. But it took three Humvees and more than a couple men to move him. Less than a minute into the mission and we were already fighting Murphy.

As Rangers and Delta operators began landing, the volume of gunfire on the objective below me increased by the second, adding to the sense of urgency up in the aircraft. I was usually the last guy out the door, but Spec. Mike Kurth, who carried the radio, had a phone cord hung up on something. *Gotta go. Gotta go now.* So I moved across to exit out the other side.

As I reached for the rope, Sergeant Ned Norton, the starboard crew chief, pointed at his head. He looked like Darth Vader with his black visor down and a dust mask covering his face. There was a red, white, and blue sticker across the front of his helmet that read "No Fear." I think Ned must have been quite proud of this sticker because he really wanted to show it to me.

"Remember!" Darth Vader yelled, pointing at his helmet. "Nooooo feeear!"

"*Screw youuuuuu!* was pretty much my reply. I grabbed the rope, took a deep breath, and disappeared out the door and into the brown abyss. I don't remember coming down the rope. I do remember the choking dust though. I looked up as the ropes were being released and Super 66 grabbed some air and disappeared. *No fear. Ha! Easy for you to say, Ned. You're flying away.*

When my feet found the street, the first thing I did was check my gear. In a previous mission, I hit hard and lost a grenade. Since it would almost certainly end up in the wrong hands, I didn't want to make that mistake again. From then on, I tied everything down. Problem solved.

I looked around to get my bearings. We were right where we needed to be, only about thirty yards from the corner of the building. I gave Doug the thumbs-up to let him know I was good to go. I then ran around the corner taking up a position across the street from the target building next to Kurth, who was getting his radio up and running.

Facing east down the narrow dirt road, I could see Lieutenant Perino's men from Chalk 1 at the next intersection. Some of them were already shooting. Sergeant Mike Goodale and Sergeant Aaron Williamson were firing from behind an old car wreck they used for cover. What were they firing at? I didn't see anybody yet.

Meanwhile to my left, I could hear the Delta assault teams moving through the target building. There is no better force in the world at clearing a building. Room to room movement in a hostile environment where bad guys are waiting to shoot you is extremely dangerous and requires incredible precision, economy of movement, lightning quick reactions, lethal accuracy, and instantaneous decision-making capabilities.

Imagine for a moment you are an important bad guy holed up in a room having an important meeting with a bunch of other important bad guys. You hear helicopters approaching. The Americans are coming. Time to go. You gather your papers and other valuables making haste to leave. Suddenly the door to your meeting room explodes wide open with a huge flash of white and a very discombobulating bang. Immediately smoke and debris fill the room.

The bodyguard next to you has an AK-47 in his hands and is raising it up to fire at something. You hear two quick and very loud gunshots—*bam! bam!*—and simultaneously that bodyguard next to you with the AK-47 collapses. What's going on? You are stunned for a second, but you know this isn't good. So you reach for a weapon leaning against the table. Bad move. *WHAM!* You are suddenly knocked to the floor with your face pressed against the concrete. You are staring straight into the eyes of the dead bodyguard who thought he was faster than the Delta operators who entered the room and are already handcuffing you.

Someone was shooting at us and getting pretty close. I couldn't get a bead on where the shooter was, but Floyd did. I think he said something like, "He's in the tree."

I couldn't really hear him, so I moved across the street to where Floyd was parked against the building. Sergeant First Class Watson, at least twenty yards away, seemed to have this crazy, acute, extrasensory perception for all things going on around him. He knew exactly what Floyd was talking about.

"Floyd!" he yelled. "Do you see him?"

"Roger, S'rgnt. He's in the tree. He's in the tree!"

"Well, Floyd, if you see him, why don't you shoot him!" It was more a suggestion than a question. As I said, the man had a way with words.

At that moment I saw a lightbulb go off just over David Floyd's Kevlar helmet accompanied by a little cartoon bubble reading, "Oh yeah! I'm a machine gunner in the 3rd Ranger Battalion! This is an M249 squad automatic weapon and I know how to use it!" Then the strangest thing happened. Suddenly the young Ranger Floyd resembled someone else entirely. Gone was the goofy, Barney Fife, "soup sandwich" of old who had a hard time meeting standards and required constant attention. In that moment Floyd figured it out. He was the one piece of the puzzle that made everything work. The lives of his platoon were on the line and everyone was counting on him to do his job and do it well 100 percent and then some. "Never shall I fail my comrades."

Floyd put his head down, charged the weapon, and sent a burst of 5.56 in the direction of our tree-borne assaulter. They teach you to fire the machine gun in a five-to-seven-round burst. So it sounds something like this, *DAT DAT DAT DAT DAT . . . DAT DAT DAT DAT DAT DAT.* You give the gun a pause in between bursts so you don't overheat the barrel. Floyd understandably was a little excited, this being his first time in combat and all. Like a Kamakazi pilot "giving" 'em the whole nine yards!" Floyd unleashed half a belt load on his target before he let his finger off the trigger.

Ranger Floyd checked his weapon, pulled up his goggles, stared at where the enemy sniper had been, and then like any, deer-hunting good ole boy would do, asked to no one in particular, "Did I get 'em?"

Now, I can't tell you if Floyd hit the guy or not. But he did get the tree. The whole thing fell over. Interesting technique and quite an effective one. Good shot, Floyd!

Tell them what you need done and they will surprise you with their results.

Goodale was directly in my line of fire, about fifty meters east of me, still shooting at an enemy I was yet to see. But another one hundred and fifty meters past him was a guy in a white robe. I don't think it was Jesus, Gandhi, or a Ku Klux Klan member, because this guy was concealing something that looked like an AK-47. He must have moved across the street at least three times before I realized what he was doing. He was spotting our positions.

Randy Ramaglia figured it too because he yelled over at me. "Hey, if you see that dude with the white robe, take him out. He's got a weapon!"

Moving target at two hundred meters. No problem. I'd done it tons of times at the moving target range back at Fort Benning. There are two techniques the Army teaches you on how to aim at a moving target. You can lead it by following with your sight and once you have a pace on its movement, you fire just in front. You can also wait for the target to come into your sight. Once it hits the leading edge of your center sight post, squeeze. Like a great golf swing, softball fast-pitch, tennis serve, or anything that requires precise aiming skills, it takes a ton of repetition. Do it enough, muscle memory will set in and it becomes second nature. Train as you fight, fight as you train.

You know as many times as I trained on moving targets and as many rounds as I fired at the shooting range, not once was Mike Goodale sitting fifty meters directly in front of where I wanted to shoot. Fortunately for Goodale, that was not part of our training. I thought, *This is gonna be a tricky shot if I have to pull it off . . . uh, oh. There he is.* The white-robed dude ran across the street again. He started moving from right to left.

Instinct and training took over as I followed him with my sights. As the target reached the leading edge of my center sight post, I squeezed and sent a round down range directly over Goodale's head who had conveniently decided to bend forward at that very moment. Man, was I glad he did because I just missed him. I almost felt guilty because I think he might have been upset with me had I shot him in the head. Next time I had to fire over Mike, I made sure to warn him first. Honestly, I still get nerves in my gut when I think about that split second. What if Goodale hadn't leaned forward? What if he sat back up at the same time I squeezed off the round?

Life is a game of inches and the line is razor thin.

"Nothing is more exhilarating than to be shot at without result." (Winston Churchill)

From my position at the target building, things were starting to get nuttier than a fruit cake. Floyd had just taken out a tree. I had just taken out Gandhi. And sporadic gunfire was beginning to pick up. All things considered though, it wasn't that bad yet. Even now as I hear myself say that, it seems absurd that someone would be shooting at us and I would think, *It's not that bad.* Can you imagine if someone fired a gun at you on your drive to work, or in your classroom, or being the day it was, Sunday, in church? That would be a big deal!

"Hey man did you hear I got shot at in the Wal-Mart parking lot? Yeah so . . . my nerves are fried and I'm taking the day off."

I think the reason I felt like being shot at by Somali militia wasn't that bad was mainly because they were missing. This would be the preferred outcome in such situations. The Somali insurgents were terrible shots and obviously lacked the training. Their bad aim was a good thing for us. But if they put enough rounds down range, sooner or later they are bound to hit something. When that's the case, do your best to make them miss. Look small and unimportant.

And that would be right about the time it hit me: Derek Jeter's baseball bat. The impact from the two 7.62mm slugs knocked me backward and left my ammunition pouch smoking. One of the bullets struck directly in the middle of the magazine that holds the rounds in what some would call a "30-round clip." It's only about an inch wide. Considering the guy who fired those rounds was at least two hundred meters away, what do you think the chances are of not one, but two rounds ricocheting off a wall, both bouncing into me and both being stopped by something less than an inch wide? Lucky shot? Lucky me? Or God? Yeah, I'll take God for $500 please, Alex.

"Do not fear them, for the LORD your God is the one fighting for you." (Deuteronomy 3:22 NASB)

If the "Lord is a Man of War" (Exod. 15:3 Amplified), I suppose every soldier, not just an American one, believes God is on his side. It follows exponentially that every big battalion must think that God is *really* on their side. And I suppose if the Pope had an army, they would consider themselves invincible.

He is a powerfully motivating force, that God of ours. History has shown how men will march forward into battle and kill each other in the name of God and country, doing what they believe to be just and right. There's the catch. What is just? Who is right when both sides believe God is on their side?

In a war of ideas, people get killed. Policies, patriotism, causes, and beliefs may be enough to send a soldier off to war. But when it comes down to it and the ideologies of the flag are gone with the wind, it is love for one another that will keep a person in the fight. If love for one another is what fighting comes down to, and God is love, then it makes sense that at a personal level, even in the midst of death and destruction, God is indeed on your side. The ideologies no longer matter. Right and wrong, God is still there for you personally and unconditionally.

"Thus says the LORD . . . Do not fear, for I have redeemed you; I have called you by name; you are Mine!" (Isaiah 43:1 NASB)

Pray for our leaders. Pray they, like Solomon, will seek wisdom. Wisdom enables leaders to make the best decision possible for the situation they have been handed. Because if the decision is made and it is deemed necessary to send your nation's best into harms way with weapons in hand, you must be prepared for the harsh fact that people are going to die. I hope that before President Clinton decided to send TFR to take out Aideed, he did a great deal of praying for wisdom and found peace in his decision.

The burden of leadership is heavy. When you are forced to make hard choices involving the lives of others—which they almost always do—make sure you have talked to God first. It's important because the people who follow you believe you. They will go where you lead. Where are you leading them and why?

The cause must be great. Being an American is usually cause enough for all who have raised their right hand and worn the uniform in defense of our nation. If a country is worth living in, then it is worth fighting for. But every side believes in their cause. Egyptian soldiers thought chasing down the Israelites was the right thing to do. They did what they were told. They followed their "enemy" right into the Red Sea, and every single one of those men died because of a bad decision on their leader's part.

Divided Americans believed so much in their specific causes, they were willing to kill each other by the tens of thousands. To this day, no war has ever produced as many American casualties as did the Civil War. In retrospect, the world can all agree Hitler was a bad man.

But in the beginning most of Germany and even Austria thought he was the answer. They didn't realize the truth until it was too late. As Sergeant Watson used to say, "There was nothing wrong with the SS. They were good troops. Just misguided."

During the Battle of the Bulge, both sides sat for months in the bitter cold, dug in, frozen, and starving. German troops and Allied Forces were but a few hundred yards apart in some places along the line. Come one Christmas Eve night, both sides could be heard singing Christmas carols celebrating the birth of Christianity. This was no religious holy war where the enemy's behavior could be dismissed as some irrational psychotic fanatical Shariah Muslim belief.

Both sides prayed to the same God and believed He was on their side. Both sides thought they were in the right. But don't think for one second any of those men fought, froze, bled, cried, and died for their God or for ideologies of right and wrong. They did it for each other, the person on their left, and the person on their right. Never shall I fail my comrades.

"When the kindness and love of God our Savior appeared, he saved us, not because of righteous things we had done, but because of his mercy."
(Titus 3:4)

Thirty-five minutes after roping in, we were wrapping up at the target house. Delta operators came out of the building with about a dozen captured men. They were the smart ones who surrendered. The prisoners were flex-cuffed, tied up, and lined up waiting for the Reaction Force to come get them with the trucks.

The "Reaction Force" was the name given to the Rangers on the vehicle element of TFR. The template plan was basic. When the helicopters took off toward the objective, the ground element would ride into the city and stage nearby the target, awaiting the word to extract. Once they got the word, they would drive up, the prisoners would be loaded, we would climb in, and we would all drive back to base. Mission accomplished.

That's pretty much how it was going. Other than Blackburn and another possibly wounded guy from Chalk 4, as far as we knew, so far so good. The lead Humvees pulled up into the intersection right where my chalk roped in. A five-ton cargo truck came along and Delta began loading the prisoners in the back.

My good friend Staff Sgt. John "JB" Burns was a squad leader in the vehicle platoon. He and I took our leaves together the year before and went down to Jamaica where we got into some trouble. But the kind of trouble one gets into on a Caribbean island sure seemed silly when compared to the given situation. Running from an old, angry Jamaican man with a machete seemed comical now that JB was running in front of his Humvee with a rocket launcher in his hand.

I knew why JB was on foot. As a Ranger, you feel more at home and more effective that way because it's what you know best. It's why we are called the infantry, soldiers who are trained to fight on foot. JB must have seen a bunch of people down the street because it looked to me like he was trying to figure out if he should fire a rocket at them or not. He had it at his side, would lift it up, have second thoughts, and consequently put it down. Obviously he was still trying to adhere to the rules of engagement.

Our rules of engagement were pretty strict. Since we would be operating in a city environment, it was imperative there were no civilian casualties. In the beginning days of TFR back at Fort Bragg during our train-up with the Delta squadron, we had a briefing to go over the rules of engagement. They began with these parameters: *You will not fire at someone unless you are fired upon.* A Somali with a weapon in hand was not necessarily a target, because practically everyone in Mogadishu carried a weapon.

We were shown photos of kids holding AK-47s and women with baskets concealing rockets for an RPG. There were photos of old Toyota pickups jammed full of people with automatic machine guns mounted in the back. The Somali militia would overload the truck to a point where they were hanging outside the bed on fabricated foot steps. We cleverly called these sort-of mounted militia "klingons." Because they were clinging. Klingons were the bad guys in Star Trek. You get it.

Do not fire at someone unless you are being fired upon.

Obviously there were a lot of imaginable scenarios where exceptions might be necessary. So understandably during the briefing there was a great deal of "what if?" questions. This is part of the planning process.

"What if someone looks like they are going to fire at you? Are we allowed to fire a warning shot?" Good question.

"What if there is a vehicle with a mounted automatic weapon that fires at us? Can we engage anyone on board even if they aren't carrying a weapon?" Another good question.

Eventually the good questions were all asked and replaced with not-so-good questions like, "What if someone points their weapon at you, tries to fire it, but it jams—so technically they didn't fire at you. Do we have to wait for them to get their weapon up and running before we return fire?"

"What if someone fired at us, then throws their weapon down and runs? Can we shoot them since they fired at us?"

"Should we wait until we see the whites of their eyes?"

When he realized this verbal volley could go on all night, the Delta team leader giving the briefing finally got tired of answering all the "what ifs." He concluded his talk by saying something that made a lasting impact on me. It's a phrase I always remember when I'm faced with a tough decision I have to make and there is no one else to give me the answer.

He said, "Look, the bottom line is this. In the chaos of battle there most likely won't be someone looking over your shoulder telling you what you can and cannot shoot at. Only you will know what you saw down the sights of your rifle. When you pull the trigger, just make sure you can live with your decision."

Fortunately JB was not willing to fire a rocket into a crowd of people and live with that decision.

Within minutes, the prisoners were loaded, and the rest of the vehicles drove off heading back to base at the airfield. The last I saw of the Humvees' was Mark Luhman. Mark was a maniac and a physical beast. He's the kind of guy you wanted on your smash-ball team, a full contact rugby-like game played with a giant pushable ball. He was up in the turret manning a .50-caliber machine gun. The vehicle stopped in the intersection, he pointed it down the street where Floyd's tree used to be, and let that big ole gun rock.

BOP BOP BOP BOP BOP BOP BOP!!

That's what you call clearing by fire. If anyone was even thinking about stepping out of an alley and taking a shot at us, those 3-inch long .50-cal rounds ripping through the air might deter them.

I remember thinking, *WOW! That thing is loud!* They must have been shot at a bunch more than us before getting here because Lou wasn't hesitating one bit.

Obviously by now the guys on the vehicles were beginning to figure out the rules of engagement established in the air-conditioned safety of a Fort Bragg briefing room were not quite applicable to the reality on the ground during a daylight raid into the heart of Indian

Country in downtown Mogadishu, Somalia. People carried weapons around for one reason. They all wanted to use them. If a Somali was anywhere near the convoy and was carrying a weapon, they were now considered a target.

It seemed to me like Luhman was still in good spirits. Just before his vehicle sped away and out of view, he looked over at me and with the sarcastic humor we all came to expect from one another, made a crazy smiley face as if to say "Can you believe this is actually going down?" That's something a person kids himself about when they are still feeling like the situation is manageable. I don't think any of us really knew what was coming next.

It took two pictures pasted together to give you an idea of how thirteen of us were packed in the Black Hawk. I took the picture while sitting on the rope. Doug Boren and Dejesus are on the left. That's SFC Watson in the middle, with Floyd and Siegler. The two crew chiefs are sitting in the windows manning the guns.

Chapter 5

LEAD, FOLLOW, OR GET OUT OF THE WAY

Never shall I fail my comrades.
—3RD STANZA OF THE RANGER CREED

"Dear Mom. You're never gonna believe what just happened. Your son is now officially a combat veteran."

Technically, this wasn't the first time TFR had been in a firefight. During one of the previous missions, some of the Rangers in the vehicles got into it briefly at their blocking position. It was a night raid, and my platoon was working at the objective pulling security for the Delta boys clearing a house.

All of a sudden from down the street, the night sky erupted in an explosion of noise and light. Tracer rounds arced across the darkness like giant taser beams reaching out to shock someone. Muzzle flashes popped off like strobe lights, and you could hear the distinctive *thump-thump-thumping* of the big .50-caliber gun over all the small arms fire. It lasted about a minute. As quickly as it started, it was over.

The rest of us literally sat in the dark wondering what just happened over there. The rest of the night was understandably tense as we peered into the shadows with our night vision knowing bad guys were out there somewhere. Though I hadn't been part of that firefight, it was a wake-up call for me about the reality of where we were and who we were up against. These people wanted to fight. They were not afraid of us.

By daybreak we made it back to the airfield and linked up with the rest of the guys. I was eager to find out what happened, so I headed over toward the vehicles and saw my buddy Steve Anderson limping toward me. He had been there at the intersection when it all went down. He was hit. A piece of shrapnel went right through his leg, which he proudly showed me like a kid bragging about a scar he got in a playground fight with the school bully. Steve was smiling.

"Look, Keni. I got shot!" Geez. Even when they hit us, they couldn't hurt us. We were supermen.

Sergeant Watson said something to us that day that made me proud. He pulled us together as a platoon and, in what seemed uncharacteristically sincere for him, he gave us a pat on the back. "Men, that was a real-world mission. Whether you realize it or not, you are now a part of the long and colorful history of the Rangers. You are all combat veterans. Good job."

Yes, his words made us feel proud of being part of Ranger history and helped to reinforce the reality of what we were sent to do. But just the same, none of us really felt like we had been in combat. We weren't the ones who fired up the bad guys. The other Rangers like Anderson who actually used their weapons, now they were in a real firefight.

But today was different. As I waited for exfiltration watching Aideed's men being escorted out of the target building, I felt different. I felt like I had finally seen it. We had been shot at. I had a couple holes in my ammunition pocket and a ding in my body armor to prove it. We had shot back. We were all leaving the field of battle with fewer rounds than we went in with. Even Floyd fired up a belt of ammo in a unique technique of sniper-in-a-tree eradication.

Combat. *So that's what it's like?* I thought. *I wonder if they'll give us a badge?*

"They have one thing you haven't got . . . a medal!"
(The Wizard to the Lion in *The Wizard of Oz*)

There were a handful of guys in the 3rd Ranger Battalion who wore a Combat Infantryman's Badge (CIB) on their uniforms. It's an old Revolutionary War silver flintlock long-rifle surrounded by a wreath of oak leaves which symbolizes "steadfast character, strength, and loyalty." According to the Army's Institute of Heraldry, a CIB can only be awarded for "being personally present, and under hostile fire, while serving in assigned, primary infantry or special forces duty in a unit actively engaging the enemy in ground combat."

Sergeant First Class Watson and Staff Sergeant Jeff Struecker were awarded their combat badges for fighting in Panama during the hunt for Manuel Noriega. There was even one man in the 3rd Ranger Battalion, Sergeant Major Ralph Borja, who wore a CIB with a star on it, meaning he'd been in combat twice. In addition to Panama, this guy was one of the original Grenada Raiders back in 1983. For those of us who had never seen a real-world mission before, we looked at these men in awe. That CIB on their uniform meant they had done the one thing we all joined the Ranger Regiment to do—go to combat.

Oh, most of us received our Expert Infantryman's Badge (EIB), a single rifle framed in light blue, which is the color of the infantry. You get to wear one on your uniform if you passed a lot of basic tasks and skills required of an "expert" infantryman. Running fast, shooting great, blowing stuff up, that was great and all. But let's face it. The ultimate test of a man was combat. A CIB, now that's a badge of honor. The EIBs we wore felt like a consolation prize handed to a game show contestant "not appearing on stage." Without the wreath, it looked like nothing more than a framed broomstick above your pocket. What a difference the little oak leaves sewn around a rifle made to those of us who knew what it meant.

A Ranger with a CIB is held by his peers at an extremely high level of esteem. More than any other award or decoration, that one demands respect because we know that he earned his badge under the most difficult missions. Rangers aren't given a CIB for riding along in the back of a tank that shot off a couple rounds from a mile away.

A CIB meant you scaled the cliffs of Point du Hoc on the beaches of Normandy. A CIB meant you were one of Merrill's Marauders who marched over the Himalayans and through the Burmese jungle to strike deep behind the Japanese lines. A CIB meant you parachuted into North Korea above the 38th parallel and fought through the freezing winter to stop the Chinese cold. A CIB meant you were Recon, patrolling the jungles of Vietnam as part of a hunter/killer team conducting long range reconnaissance into hostile territory with nothing more than you could carry on your back. A CIB meant you were a storm trooper liberator who parachuted under fire in a daring low level combat assault jump into Grenada or Panama. A CIB means you are the tip of the spear in the war on terror taking down the enemy in the very heart of Iraq or way out in the most remote parts of the Afghani mountains. To those of us who had never worn one, a CIB over your heart meant you were part of the long and colorful history of the 75th Ranger Regiment. It meant you were a warrior, and God was surely on the side of a warrior.

"The LORD is a warrior; the LORD is his name."
(Exodus 15:3)

Badges should mean something to those who wear them. I have the opportunity to speak and perform for Boy and Girl Scouts fund-raisers around the nation. Usually there is a boy or girl who is honored at the event for a significant achievement of the highest order. A young man has shown the intestinal fortitude required to complete all the tasks required to earn his Eagle Scout badge. A young lady is presented with the Girl Scouts Gold award. This is a big deal.

You can feel the pride in the room as their accolades are read for all to hear. The kid stands there on the stage looking a little uncomfortable. Someone of some local importance shakes their hand and pins on the medal. The recipient says, "Thank you," and the presenter steps away and the crowd begins to cheer. I'm usually right by the stage, so I get to see up close what always happens next.

Without fail, as the crowd applauds in appreciation, that kid who is now standing a little straighter and taller, looks at the award hanging from their uniform. They reach down and touch it, as if to verify that, yes, their dream is finally realized. And then, oblivious to the crowd, they smile to themselves, lost for a moment in the thought of all it took to get where they are.

For all their years of hard work, dedication, and commitment to excellence, do we give these exceptional young people real gold, money, a college scholarship, or even a gift certificate to Applebees? Nope. They are given only a badge, a piece of cloth and tin. But that little badge speaks volumes about that person. It screams out to the world, "Look! Look! Look what I have done!" For all those who have donned the badge before you, they will recognize what it means and appreciate its significance. Others will envy, admire, and be inspired by it.

I love being in attendance at events like that. Watching someone receive an award is motivating. I believe the ceremony is important. Even if it's just gathering your coworkers together in the office to recognize someone for their accomplishment, a ceremony instills pride and reinforces a commitment to higher achievement. We are Americans. We love overachievers!

Hang a medal around your neck. Sew a badge on your uniform. Frame a diploma and put it in your office. Run home to show your mom the gold star on your hand. To do these things means you have become extraordinary and you know what it feels like to be a part of something much larger than yourself. Do these things, and you have become a proud member of an exclusive club no amount of money will get you into. Only hard work and accomplishment can gain you access. Sure you could go out and buy a symbol of your achievement. But that's not the same as being awarded one now, is it? That title you are wearing, that little insignia you have sewn on your shoulder, there are many like it. But that one is yours. You should be proud because you have earned the right to wear it. Now here comes the hard part. You're gonna have to live up to it.

There is a scene in the movie *A Few Good Men* where Tom Cruise's character Dan Kaffee, a young cocky Navy JAG officer, is trying to counsel a hard-headed Marine named Harold who refuses to compromise. Harold believes if he accepts the plea bargain the prosecution is offering, he will be stripped of his title as a U.S. Marine and thus his honor as a man. Kaffee wisely tells Harold that "you don't need a patch on your arm to have honor."

It isn't the gold medal that makes an Olympian a champion. It isn't the ranger tab that makes a Ranger. It's not the piece of red, white, and blue cloth with a silver star hanging from it that makes a man a hero. It isn't the diploma, the hat, the badge, the name tag, or the commemorative pin that differentiates you from the norm and earns you respect as a leader. It is the example you set. That is the real badge of honor. I do not wear a cross on my guitar strap to brag to everyone I am a Christian. I wear it as a reminder to myself that I have chosen a path that requires an example to be set and people are watching.

"Gallantly will I show the world that I am a specially selected and well-trained soldier." (from the 5th stanza of the Ranger Creed)

Combat veteran. Yep, I thought as a few stray rounds fired over our heads. I think this time we earned that title. Maybe I'll get that CIB after all and this time really become "part of the long and colorful history of the Ranger Regiment."

For the most part, the mission was just about done. We successfully raided the building and caught the people we were after. The Delta operators captured a dozen of Aideed's men including

Mohammed Hassan Awale and Omar Salad Elmi, who were top priorities on our most-wanted list. The Reaction Force drove up, loaded the prisoners, and sped off toward the compound back at the airfield. The rest of us in the "Assault Force" on the objective were waiting for our ride home. A couple minutes after that, we got the word one of the five-ton trucks coming to get us had been hit with an RPG. Apparently they were bringing in another one. We would be waiting a little longer than planned.

Hit by an RPG? How bad? I wondered. I hope the guys on the truck are OK. No one said anything about casualties on the radio, so I'm sure they're OK. Remember we had a superman mentality. Nothing could hurt us. We were the Rangers. We had Delta and Navy SEALs on our side. The Night Stalkers had our backs. If an RPG hit a truck, it probably just disabled it.

Dear Mom, I went back to imagining. *Great news. Now that I'm a combat veteran, I bet I can qualify for a VA loan!* I figured these were the things a mom would rather hear about instead of "Dear Mom, I got shot." It had been a day off from training. We weren't even supposed to be working. And just like that, we got the call that would turn us into the combat veterans we all wanted to be. The mission was a success. The raid was done. We got the bad guys. We were waiting to go home. End of story. I was already patting myself on the back thinking, *Man, if my friends could see me now.*

And just like that, everything changed.

We all saw it smoking. Super 61 had been flying low and slow in an over-watch flight pattern when it was hit in the tail boom by a rocket propelled grenade. It turned a slow 360 in what seemed to be a somewhat controlled maneuver, but not really. The MH-60 was starting its autorotation, the automatic procedure for crash landings. Everyone knew what it meant, but none of us could believe it. That's not supposed to happen. That's the 160th up there. No way did a third-world clan of thugs and poorly trained klingons riding on the back of Toyota trucks wearing flip-flops and football helmets just bring down the best of the best. But there it was, right before our eyes. The aircraft lost altitude and disappeared into the buildings about a half mile to the northeast.

The radio exploded in a high-pitched oration as someone frantically reported what we already were well aware of. They were the words that would one day come to define this battle, make Mark Bowden famous and Ridley Scott rich. "We have a Black Hawk going down. We got a Black Hawk going down. We've got a Black Hawk crashed in the city."

The mission changed. We had a Black Hawk down and we had to get to that crew before the rest of the city did. If we didn't, the guys on board who might still be alive were doomed.

We all knew what happened to the crews of a downed helicopter. A few weeks earlier a UH-60 from another unit crash-landed in the middle of the city. No one was there to help those guys. The crew was overrun and literally torn to pieces. A few days later we watched from our compound as the bodies of those Americans were loaded in stainless steel coffins into the back of a C-5 transport. I thought to myself, *That's never going to happen to our guys. We won't let it. Besides, we have the Night Stalkers. And they don't get shot down.*

"In a war more than anywhere else in the world,
things happen differently from what we
had expected and look different when near
from what they did at a distance."
(Karl Van Clausewitz)

It felt like an eternity before a decision was made that we would move to the crash site on foot. Why was this taking so long?

Let's go! Let's go! Let's go NOW!

You know in the movies when there's a fire in a building and you see a mother who desperately wants to run in and save her child from the flames, but the fireman won't let her go and holds her back? That's what it felt like. Fear. Anger. Helplessness. Frustration. Time is running out. Trust me, it's exactly how you would feel if you were put into the same type situation.

What if you are standing on the street corner at a busy intersection and you see a friend of yours in a bad car crash right in front of you? You are going to instinctively run to help. But as any EMT or paramedic will tell you, the first thing you have to do is make a quick assessment of the situation at hand. Are there cars coming? Have you looked both ways before running out into the street? Don't go off half-cocked and end up a casualty yourself becoming part of the problem.

So the people in charge had to make a quick assessment of the situation, and we had to come to grips with the reality of the cards we were just dealt. It wasn't right. It wasn't fair. You don't have to be happy about it, but what are you going to do about it? Fortunately we planned for this type of situation. We trained on this exact scenario.

In the highly unlikely event of a helicopter going down, here's what we rehearsed. If the crash is nearby, the ground force would move on foot to the crash site and extract the crew. The Humvees would come to assist with evacuation. On every mission, just in case and without exception, a combat search and rescue team (CSAR) would be in the air on constant standby.

CSAR had to be a crappy job. While the rest of TFR flew off for a mission or drove away in their gun trucks, you had to cram yourself into the cargo bay of a MH-60 Black Hawk with fifteen other men knowing you were just going to fly around in circles for an hour while everyone else got to do the real deal down on the objective. I know what I would have been thinking. *Man, this sucks. I'm never gonna get to do anything during this deployment because there's just no way anyone from the 160th is gonna get shot down.*

But the men who made up the CSAR team took their jobs very seriously. Air Force PJs like Tech Sgt. Tim Wilkerson and Tech Sgt. Scott Fales were absolute experts. Rangers like Sgt. First Class Al Lamb, Sgt. Alan Barton and Sgt. John Bellman who were assigned to pull security for the PJs, were as good as they came.

They all understood, that should the need arise, CSAR was the most critical asset available to TFR. Sergeant First Class Lamb knew he and his Rangers were the one piece of the puzzle that made everything work. Without them, the PJs could not tend to the wounded. Lives would be lost when they could have been saved. That is something none of us could ever live with. "Never shall I fail my comrades." So the CSAR guys trained and they trained and they trained, knowing that if all went as it should, they would never be needed. But one day, just like that, everything for those men changed.

I have seen the video feed taken from the reconnaissance aircraft circling overhead. I wish that one day it could be made public so everyone can see and be inspired by the incredible bravery that took place in those critical minutes after the crash. Super 61 slammed into an alley and came to rest on its left side with the nose crushed up against a wall. The two pilots Chief Warrant Officers Cliff "Elvis" Wolcott and Donovan "Bull" Briley were both killed on impact when the cockpit collapsed around them. The two crew chiefs, Staff Sgts. Ray Dowdy and Charlie Warren, would survive the ground collision as did the two Delta snipers who had spread-eagled themselves on the floor to try and absorb some of the spine-crushing impact. As the dust began to settle, you could see two of the Delta operators stumble from the wreckage. It was Sergeant First Class Jim Smith and Staff Sergeant Dan Busch.

Dan was the first out and immediately began to engage the enemy who had already begun coming around the corner. We knew Staff Sergeant Busch better than the other D-boys because he was once one of our own. He was a squad leader with Bravo Company before going to Delta selection. Dan Busch was living proof that if we aspired to be part of the elite Delta Force, it could indeed be done.

Dan Busch was in a fight for his life and every skill he ever learned as a Delta shooter was now in full survival mode. There were Somalis everywhere in all directions. He moved to the corner of the nearby intersection and fired round after round at the oncoming armed mob. Then as if someone quietly told him to stop, Dan Busch ceased shooting and leaned back against the wall. He had been shot in the stomach. Sergeant First Class Smith, the other operator who made it out of the crash, ran to Dan's side.

Busch and Smith moved about thirty yards from the crash to an open four-way cross road when Dan was shot. Help arrived in an unlikely fashion, when a couple minutes later an MH-6 Little Bird, call sign "Star 41," made a daring and seemingly impossible landing. Instead of setting down in the middle of the intersection and becoming a big fat target, the Little Bird squeezed itself into the alley where it could at least have some cover from two sides. This was no simple feat given the tight space available to maneuver that aircraft.

But the Night Stalkers at the controls were the best helicopter fliers in the world. I once saw them chase a car through the streets below rooftop level. As long as there was space for the rotors, these guys could make the impossible work. Star 41 set down and immediately came under fire. The pilot, Chief Warrant Officer 4 Keith Jones, jumped from the cockpit and sprinted out into the firefight to help Smith drag the bleeding Dan Busch back into the aircraft. All the while, the copilot Chief Warrant Officer 3 Karl Maier held the aircraft steady on the ground with one hand and with the other covered his comrades by firing his side arm out of the door at the advancing enemy. Chief Jones loaded the wounded operator into the small space behind the seats, pulled Sergeant Smith in with him, got back in the driver's seat and Star 41 lifted away.

It was at that exact moment when Lieutenant Tom DiTomasso and his Chalk 2 Rangers arrived on the scene. They had seen the bird go down and happened to have a direct line of sight to the crash when no one else did. Remember Chalk 4 that got roped in 100 yards too soon? That was the helicopter Blackburn had fallen from. When Lt. DiTomasso got word that Chalk 4 was in the wrong place, he immediately moved to link up with them so that they would not be left out there all alone. DiTomasso and his men were en route to help when the helicopter crashed into the very same street they were moving down. Tom will tell you the story quite clearly with total recall.

"We were en route to link up with Sergeant Eversmann's Chalk 4. Movement was slow because we were meeting some resistance. In fact we were fighting from inside a building and had taken a couple prisoners when Joe Thomas my FO came running in saying he had just seen a helicopter get shot down and he knew where it was."

Obviously the mission had just changed. So Lt. DiTomasso called in his new position explaining he had a direct line of sight and was now en route to the crash instead. He also had an immediate understanding of the dire situation at hand, because he could see what was going on when no one else in our chain of command could.

But surprisingly he was told by Captain Steele, "Do not move." Tom DiTomasso had a leadership decision to make.

"When I looked at the crowd of Somalis who were now sprinting towards the crash, I knew we had no choice. If any one of our guys was still alive, they were going to need our help. I looked at the men I trusted looking back at me, and they all agreed, we had to move and move fast," Tom explained.

Lt. DiTomasso left half of his Chalk 2 there to complete the link up with Eversmann's Chalk 4. And then, ignoring the orders to stay put, he and the rest of his men sprinted east to help their fallen comrades. They got there just before the Little Bird, Star 41, lifted away with the two wounded Delta operators.

Tom tells this next part of the story with a bit of sarcastic amusement in his voice. It's one of those moments you can laugh about after the fact, after it all works out OK.

"When we got to the intersection I certainly didn't expect to see a Little Bird, sitting there too. Karl Maier, the pilot, was just as surprised I think. He was sitting in the cockpit firing out the window at the crowd of people to the north. I must have startled him because he turned his weapon and pointed it right at me! I'm glad he was paying attention and didn't pull the trigger. I could see Keith Jones dragging the two wounded Delta operators into the other side of the bird so I tapped my head at Karl indicating a "head count." I wanted to know if they had gotten everyone out of the crash. He shook his head no and then Star 41 took off."

As the Little Bird lifted up out of the intersection, DiTomasso got his first real look at the wreckage of Super 61. The same Somali crowd he and his men had seen racing down the street had beaten them there and were already attacking the survivors.

"One of the crew chiefs was stumbling out into the street covering his face because people were beating him with sticks and rocks," Tom recalls. It was a good thing we got there when we did because neither he nor the other crew chief who was still alive would have made it."

Within minutes Super 68 was on the scene to insert Al Lamb's 15-man CSAR team. The Black Hawk hovered over the intersection, ropes went out, and the men start heading to the ground.

"At first I didn't know what was happening," Tom told me. "I got knocked to my knees and started choking on the dust. I looked up and saw Rangers everywhere. The CSAR team was roping in directly over our heads."

The most vulnerable time for our Black Hawks was during insertion while ropes were out. It's a dangerous time for the Rangers too because four of the men on the CSAR team got hit coming down the rope. And sure enough, Super 68 was hammered with an RPG right in the rotors. The guy showing us the tape rewound it and pointed out the impact. Instinct would cause a pilot to react and fly away. But Chief Warrant Officer Dan Jollota and Major Herb Rodriguez had the presence of mind to hold that bird together because men were still on the ropes. Lives were squarely in their hands. When the last man hit the ground, the crew chief cut the ropes and gave the call, "ropes away." Then and only then did Dan Jollota pull out and nurse his helicopter back toward the air base. After a controlled crash landing, the crew ran on foot back to the airfield, jumped into the only spare Black Hawk available, and rejoined the fight. Both pilots would later be awarded the Distinguished Flying Cross for their incredible efforts that day.

From the moment they got the word Super 61 went down, it took less than three minutes for every single one of those men on the CSAR team to get out of the sky and onto the ground to set up a defensive perimeter around that crash site. Just think. Five minutes earlier, they were crammed into the cargo bay thinking they would probably never be needed.

Both pilots were dead. Two crew chiefs were hurt. Four men from the CSAR team were wounded. And Somalis throwing grenades and shooting bullets were everywhere. Even with the added CSAR team, Lt. DiTomasso knew he needed more men. So he called the rest of his guys up that he had left back down the street. His men took up a perimeter covering the intersection, enabling Al Lamb's CSAR team to get into position and get to work saving the wounded. They would stay there fighting off a tenacious enemy the entire night.

After inserting his chalk of Rangers on the initial raid, Mike Durant the pilot of Super 64 was placed in a holding pattern outside the city. At that point he was thinking the same thing as the CSAR guys, that he would probably not be needed either. Right up until Cliff Wolcott's Black Hawk was shot down.

Someone had to fill the void in the over-watch position. A few minutes later Super 64 got the call. Mike banked his aircraft toward the objective as Star 41 was lifting off the street at the crash and Dan Jollota was inserting the CSAR team. Mike hardly had time to get his bearings when he too was hit with an RPG in the tail rotor. Super 64 never made it back. They crashed into a shanty shack neighborhood about a mile south of where we were.

In short succession and in the span of five minutes, five souls were lost and over thirty million dollars of sophistication were shot out of the sky by a grossly underestimated enemy armed with a rudimentary weapon that costs less than a tank of gas. What was it again that David used to take down Goliath?

There is something disturbingly calm about watching a battle unfold on a live black and white aerial feed. There is no sense of urgency. No sound. No explosion. No warning buzzers in the cockpit. No gunfire. No ringing in the ears. No centrifugal force felt as your aircraft corkscrews toward the earth. No recoil of the rifle. No dust, dirt, and sweat in the eyes. No pain felt when the man you are watching gets hit and stumbles. Then gets hit again, stumbles, and collapses to the ground. Based on what they are seeing from a view that looks to be about a hundred feet up, I don't see how anyone in a command center can feel the urgency and sensory overload a soldier feels in the fight.

"A picture's worth a thousand words but you can't see what those shades of gray keep covered. You should have seen it in color." (from the song "In Color" by Jamey Johnson)

Meanwhile back at the objective, waiting for the word to move was painful and taking way too long. In real time, however, it only took about seven minutes. We were given the location of the crash, a direction, and an order of movement. The bird went down only five blocks away, three blocks east and two blocks north. So we would head east down the street toward where I saw the white-robed-Gandhi-dude with a weapon, then turn left toward the crash. About seventy of us Rangers and Delta alike would move tactically as a group, down both sides of the street at a quick but controlled pace spread out in five-meter intervals.

Just before we got ready to move out, Doug Boren, my buddy from Texas and our squad leader, went running into the target building where the medic was set up. Doug was holding his neck, and from what I could see, was bleeding pretty bad. Sergeant First Class Watson followed him in and a few minutes later came out and informed me, "Boren's been hit. You're in charge."

"Is he all right, S'rgnt?"

"He's been hit. You're in charge."

"Yeah, but what happened? Is he gonna be OK?"

Sergeant Watson stopped me right there.

"Sergeant Thomas, you're in charge!"

I got it. He was right.

I did not ask for that responsibility. I did not ask for that to happen. *I'm not even sure I'm ready for this.* It may not be fair. But there it is. So what are you gonna do about it? The answer was simple. There were people counting on me. It was time to lead.

Fortunately I knew what to do because we planned for it and trained for it. I took Doug's radio and clipped it to my hip then turned to Dejesus. "You're the team leader now buddy."

I saw that street-hard fire in his eyes, "Roger, Sgt! In Puerto Rico, everyone is a team leader!" Man, I'm glad that guy was on my side.

"Floyd, look after Suranski. Suranski, look after Floyd. Do what you know is right and we'll be just fine. Follow me!"

By this time the four of us were the absolute last to move out in a long line of men heading down both sides of the streets. Sergeant First Class Watson stayed with us and we brought up the rear. Doug went on ahead with Bart the Delta medic. I figured they would get him bandaged up and get him medevaced out to someplace safe. Someplace safe. What was I thinking?

It was becoming a foot race. As we passed alleys and crossed intersections, you could see Somalis running down adjacent streets in the same direction we were going. As I sprinted to catch up to the main element ahead of us, my mind was racing with thoughts of those silver coffins of the unfortunate helicopter crew from the 10th Mountain who had crashed on these streets weeks earlier. *I sure hope we get there in time.*

"In forty hours I shall be in battle, with little information, and on the spur of the moment will have to make the most momentous decisions. But I believe that one's spirit enlarges with responsibility and that, with God's help, I shall make them and make them right." (General George Patton)

Fortunately the crash site was in good hands. The CSAR team was in place and reinforced by Tom DiTomasso's Chalk 2. Four men on board Super 61 had survived the crash. The two Delta snipers fighting alone in the streets had been pulled out and evacuated by the heroics of the Star 41 Little Bird pilots who landed their aircraft where an aircraft could not be landed. No one had told Chief Jones and Chief Maier to do what they did. It just needed to be done. And they knew if not them, then who?

Moments after that the CSAR team was inserted, they came under full attack. They needed help. But as God would have it, Lieutenant Tom DiTomasso and his Chalk 2 group of Rangers were exactly where they needed to be, at the exact time they needed to be there. Despite previous instructions from higher up to stay where he was, Lieutenant DiTomasso made a *sua sponte* decision and moved out right away. He did not wait. He did not hesitate. It was a good thing he did what he did. The two crew chiefs, Staff Sgts. Ray Dowdy and Charlie Warren, who were overwhelmed by an angry mob are still alive today because of Tom DiTomasso's ability to make a decision and to do what needed to be done.

For his actions that day, First Lieutenant Tom DiTomasso would later be awarded the Silver Star. He was also fired. Captain Steele let his best platoon leader go for having disobeyed the order "Do not move." It was a terrible leadership decision on Captain Steele's part, selfish and misguided. Put in Lt. DiTomasso's shoes, every single one of us would have done the same. In fact, Tom will tell you himself that if he had the chance to do it all over again, he would, without hesitation, do the exact same thing. He can also tell you in one sentence what it's taken me an entire book to say.

"As a leader, you do the right thing, because it's the right thing to do. I know in my heart it was the right decision because the men that I trusted most, the ones to my left and to my right, have told me so."

Amen, Tom.

Sometimes the burden of leadership requires hard choices to be made based upon difficult situations with a lot less information than you would like. And sometimes the right decisions will not always work out in your personal favor. When the level of immediacy is pegging into the red and the sense of urgency is over the top, there can be no waffling or "What should I do? Maybe we should have a meeting." A course of action must be decided upon quickly and decisively. If you are the Washington Generals, you have the entire off-season to figure out how to finally beat the Harlem Globetrotters. But if you are Tom DiTomasso and lives are on the line, you have but moments.

"Sua sponte (of their own accord)"
(motto of the 75th Ranger Regiment)

I frequently get to speak to students at the Air Force Academy. It's one of the coolest events I do. These cadets are some of the brightest and most motivated young men and women I've ever met on a college campus. They know exactly what they have signed on for; currently there is a war on two fronts in which they will most likely have to serve. One day soon they will be thrust into a leadership role, put in charge of people much more experienced than they are and be expected to make good decisions and do it better than most because of that Air Force Academy ring they wear. Since we are all bound to make mistakes, especially as a new lieutenant, I tell them this.

"Good leaders are expected to make tough decisions. You're not always expected to be right. It's OK to be wrong. As long as I know you are making an effort to learn from your mistakes and better the team, I will continue to follow you. The important thing is to make a decision. The best leaders make the best decisions they can based on the situation. The worst leaders make no decisions at all. You lead, you follow, or get out of the way."

I'm always disappointed by someone who feels like they need to have yet another meeting to decide on a course of action that does not require a group consensus. If you have all the information and you know your abilities, then make a decision. Lead, follow, or get out of the way. Don't be part of the problem. Be part of the solution.

Moses had the huge burden of leading his people across a desert. They were en route to Canaan, the land of milk and honey God promised to the Jewish people. After years of trudging along in a nomadic existence, they finally made it to the Jordan River valley. The Promised Land was just on the other side. Much to the unpopularity of his impatient followers, Moses decided to hole up in the hills and assess the situation before sending everyone across the river. He knew the people who inhabited the land were not going to give it up without a fight. So Moses sent in a twelve-man reconnaissance team to put eyes on the objective and see what they were up against.

The twelve spies of Israel, as they became known, were one man assigned from each tribe. Their instructions were to go into Canaan and scout it out. Moses wanted specifics. What are the strengths and numbers of the current inhabitants? What's the terrain like? Is the land fertile? And by the way bring us back some fruit if you can. I thought the fruit was a good call seeing as how they'd been living on manna bread for years. (And I thought MREs were bad.) After forty days the spies return with their report.

Apparently Canaan was a lot like Texas. Everything was big. The grapes. The valley. The cities. Even the inhabitants were described as giants. Most of the spies were afraid, saying, "We were like grasshoppers in their sight." All the spies agreed about the goodness of the land but only two, Joshua and Caleb, believed the job of taking Canaan could be accomplished. Their reasoning was sound. "Hey, we have God on our side. If He said it can be done, then it can be done." The other ten were not so sure. They were too afraid of the giant Texans and advised Moses not to try and take Canaan.

Well Moses did what any good leader would do. He listened to the information available and then made a decision. Obviously Moses was going with God. He agreed with Joshua who told everyone, "The Lord is with us. Do not be afraid."

You can lead a horse to water, but you can't make him drink. The ten disgruntled spies weren't listening and begin spreading rumors among the people about the impossible odds stacked against them. Fear is a powerful force if not kept in check. The people panicked, abandoning their faith, saying, "We'd rather die in the desert of Egypt than go into the Promised Land." After everything Moses did to lead them that far, after everything God did to keep them alive and get them thus far, the ungrateful cowards no longer wanted to follow.

So God gave them exactly what they asked for. Every single one of them over the age of twenty died in the desert where they were sentenced to wander for forty years, one year for every day the spies had been gone. Joshua would assume command from Moses and eventually lead the next generation of Israelites across the river and into Canaan defeating the "giants" and securing the land God promised them.

The point is, a great leader like yourself must be able to make a decision, then act upon it, even if it is contradictory to what the majority may or may not be telling you. But remember, tough leadership decisions do not always have happy endings. Some people may praise your decision, while others will most certainly find fault in your logic. You may not always be patted on the back for doing the right thing. Sometimes you might even be persecuted, ridiculed, spat upon, tortured, and hung on a cross. At the end of the day, you have to live with yourself and the choices you make. Only you know what you see down the sights of your rifle. If right is on your side, then lead the way!

"The LORD is with us. Do not be afraid of them."
(Numbers 14:9)

Suranski looked confused. It didn't seem to me he was making good decisions. As we moved toward the crash site, we would pause at the intersections to pull security as each man took their turn crossing one at a time. Basically, it takes three people to cross a road. One person on each side of the road kneels down and pulls security in opposite directions to cover for the one guy crossing. Once he gets to the other side, he then takes the place of the person waiting for him and covers for the next guy coming across. We called it "scroll to the road." This was a foolproof method of ensuring a Ranger would never forget which way to face down the street when it was his turn to pull security. The 3rd Ranger Battalion scroll was sewn onto your right shoulder. Keep your "scroll to the road" and you were always facing the right direction. If it's stupid but works, it isn't stupid.

It was our turn to cross and since I was leading my group of four, I would go first. The guy across the street was a Delta operator, Sergeant First Class Fillmore. He was on a knee patiently waiting for us to catch up to the main group. He knew I was counting on him to cross the street safely so he held his position longer than he would of liked. Suranski was behind me so he would cover this side of the street. But instead of taking a knee, Private Suranski simply stayed standing up. Not once in any of our training had we taught him it was OK to stand up while pulling security during a scroll to the road.

Suranski was letting the stress of the situation cloud his thought process. I yelled at him to get down. Once he got across to me, as calmly as I could manage, I told him, "Look. I don't want to have to start stressing you out, man. Don't mean to yell, but you have got to do what you know is right. Stay down. Spread out. OK?"

"Roger, S'rgt," he said. He sure seemed much calmer than his actions had just shown.

It was weird, but right at that moment, I picked up a date that fell off an abandoned fruit cart and took a bite. I offered him one. I tried to smile to ease his mind.

"Date?"

I found that moment amusing because it came straight out of a fable I heard once about a tiger and a strawberry. A man was running from a tiger and jumped out over a cliff. Hanging from a vine he looked over and saw a big fat strawberry that ended up being the most delicious natural snack he'd ever tasted. The lesson was supposed to be about the little beautiful things that are still present even when our lives are seemingly overwhelmed. *Well,* I thought, *whoever wrote that story might have been chased by a tiger. But they were never chased and fired at by Somali militia, because that date didn't taste delicious at all.*

Obviously Suranski hadn't heard of the tiger and the strawberry nor did he find it amusing because he just shook his head as if to say "What? Are you kidding me?" I think I might have appeared a lot calmer than I was.

Every now and then, Dejesus and I would fire back down the street from where we had just come, because we could see small groups of armed men following us. But up ahead, it looked like our people were having a hard time making the left turn. The formation was beginning to bunch up along the wall. And now we were stopped. Sergeant First Class Watson, who was bringing up the rear, was understandably concerned about the gunmen who were following us. He wanted our train to get going.

"Sergeant Thomas. Move around the corner."

"I can't, S'rgt, we're all bogged down."

You know how a parent knows exactly when to use that certain tone in their voice? You know the one. It's the tone that gets results. While talking very deliberately, they annunciate every single syllable so as to make themselves perfectly clear. Sergeant Watson repeated the command.

"Sergeant Thomas! MOVE . . . AROUND . . . THE CORNER!"

"Roger that."

I think Ramaglia even felt the heat because he was on the other side of the street hollering at the CO to get moving. Sometimes if you "yell more loudlier, it moves things more quicklier!"

Once we made the left-hand turn around the building, I then saw what the holdup was. The streets exploded into a full-on firefight. Tracer rounds were coming and going down the middle of the road. Rangers were shooting. Delta was shooting. Little Birds were shooting. Somalis were shooting. Seemed like the entire city was shooting. Even the noise level instantly increased from stereo to full-blown surround sound cranked to 11.

At that point, it was what we called "Hollywood." Because the only place you ever saw anything like this was in the movies.

The four platoon leaders of B company—Lt. Scott Spellmeyer, Lt. Tom DiTomasso, Lt. Larry Perino, and Lt. Larry Moore

Chapter 6

HOLLYWOOD

Readily will I display the intestinal fortitude required
to fight on to the Ranger objective and complete
the mission though I be the lone survivor.
—6TH STANZA OF THE RANGER CREED

MEL GIBSON WOULD NOT TIE his boot laces. I was constantly tucking them in for him.

"Keni. Don't worry about it. They won't be on camera."

"But you're the colonel," I told him. "Everyone is looking at you. I've got two hundred extras I'm trying to make look and act like soldiers. Let's try and set an example for others to follow."

I got to spend a few months helping out as one of the military advisors on the set of *We Were Soldiers*. It was the movie version of a battle recounted in the book *We Were Soldiers Once . . . and Young* by

Joe Galloway and Hal Moore. In November of 1965 during the early years of the Vietnam War, a battalion of about 450 American troopers from the 7th Cavalry air assaulted into the Ia Drang Valley near the border of North Vietnam. They went out on a search and destroy mission. What they didn't know was they were inserted smack in the middle of an entire regiment of 2,000 North Vietnamese Army regulars. Surrounded and outnumbered, the American soldiers fought for two days to keep each other alive.

There was a scene we were shooting that took place in a foxhole at night. Mel Gibson, who plays Lieutenant Colonel Hal Moore, is moving up and down the line to check in with and reassure his men. They are scared and anxious, staring out into the darkness waiting for the impending attack. Director Randy Wallace wanted to use me in the shot so he puts me in the foxhole and then leaned down to give me some acting guidance on the scene. Randy was a wonderful and sincere man, but at that point, he was being a little sarcastic.

"Now, Keni, I know you probably don't know anything about what it's like to be in combat. So I want you to try real hard and imagine, if you can, what it might feel like to be scared, outnumbered, and surrounded. OK?"

Hmm. Let me see if I can do that for you, Randy.

"Annnnnddd . . . ACTION!"

WHACK! Whoa, that was close.

A bullet going by you makes a very distinctive sound, sort of like someone slapping two boards together right by your head. When it's close enough, you can actually feel the percussion as the subsonic projectile rips a path through the air. I had barely turned the corner when what they call an "unfriendly" round went by. The term "unfriendly" seems ridiculously understated and unnecessary to me. I don't care who pulled the trigger, friend or foe, any round coming at you should always be considered unfriendly and downright . . . *deadly*.

Keep moving. Speed was security. The problem was when we made that left-hand turn north toward the crash, everything bogged down and backed up like a five o'clock traffic jam. Forward movement came to a halt.

Super 61 wedged itself on impact in a small alley about two blocks up on the right. The CSAR rescue squad and Lieutenant DiTomasso's Rangers had already put up a defensive perimeter around the downed aircraft. With Somali militia coming in all directions, the rest of the Rangers and Delta operators were intermixed in pockets of fighting on both sides of the streets all along this two-block length. By the time my squad turned the corner, there wasn't much more room to maneuver. I pushed my men in about thirty yards to the first cross street. We were now the link to the rest of the force up ahead. Sergeant First Class Watson and his element filled in the space behind me and I ran back and forth relaying the situation to him.

I couldn't get over the volume of fire going on around me. It was just so impressive. M16s and AK-47s were popping. Machine guns were rocking on full automatic. Tracer rounds were zipping down the street. Unfriendly rounds were cracking and impacting from all directions. The noise got so deafening my ears must have just shut down because other than that initial shock to my senses, I honestly can't recall hearing much of anything after that. But if you've ever been around any sort of weapon when it goes off, you know it's loud. Multiply that by a hundred and you've almost got an idea of how it was.

Still, it felt like training. Shoot. Move. Communicate. First thing you do is to put your men in a good position that provides adequate cover and concealment. Since concealment was pretty much null and void out there in the street, the best you could do was to find some cover then assign each man an effective field of overlapping fire. My guys were now facing back west toward the target building watching the same road I saw so many Somalis running down during our footrace to the crash.

Once you had your positions assigned, next thing you did was to scan your sector of fire, identify a target, and remember your rules of engagement. It was tricky. There were Somali people darting around everywhere. At one point we saw a gunman dash across the road and into an alley. So we watched that area. Seconds later a heavy woman and two teenage kids came running out from the very same spot. I'm thinking she looked awfully well-fed.

I thought these people were starving.

I fired a couple warning shots over their heads. They really needed to get out of here and not come back less they get caught in the cross fire.

Hey . . . there she is again. What is she doing?

What we figured out is the Somalis were using women and children to spot our positions. They knew our rules of engagement. They knew we would not fire at an unarmed woman, so they sent them out into the street as spies. That's exactly what the fat lady was doing. She would run around for a second, then disappear out of our view to tell the shooter where we were. The shooter would then step out, fire a burst from his rifle or send an RPG our way. A few minutes later she would show up again running down the street. Maybe she thought we wouldn't recognize her. But a fat lady in Somalia stands out like a Ranger in Mogadishu.

After a couple times of playing this game, I knew what was coming next. I'd watch the alley or the door she disappeared into and then waited. Sure enough a shooter would step out making the decision to pull the trigger an easy one for me.

If you think you have to shoot, you want to make certain you know what you are shooting at. Are you only firing warning shots or is it a real threat? How do you know? You look at their hands. At this point in the battle, if the enemy had a weapon in their hands, they were considered a threat and thus a target. In that case, aim center mass. Breathe. Squeeze. Identify another target. I felt I had this under control. Train as you fight. Fight as you train.

It was training right up until I heard the screaming.

I've never heard a man scream like that. In fact, I've never heard anything like that. It was the sound of a human in terrible pain. It cuts through all the noise and instantly sucks you into a whole new level of reality.

His name was Sergeant First Class Earl Fillmore. He was the Delta operator who helped my team cross the road about ten minutes earlier. Sergeant Fillmore was moving down the street directly across from me when he was hit in the head. My friend Mike Kurth who was on that side of the street said he saw Fillmore's head snap back as a small puff of red came out the back of Earl's helmet. The Delta operators didn't wear the heavy Kevlar "K pots" we had. They wore lightweight plastic hockey style helmets that did absolutely nothing to stop a bullet.

One of Fillmore's buddies was right there and immediately moved to help, but then that man got hit too. I was confused because I couldn't tell if the screaming was from Earl or this other guy. I only know I wanted it to stop. The wounded operator was desperate to remedy the situation. He was shouting at me to help find a way to get

Sergeant Fillmore off the street and into the hands of someone who could fix him and make it right again.

"We need to get him medevaced. It's a head shot!" he yelled.

I ran back to Watson, who had control of a radio and therefore could communicate with a higher-up. Sergeant Watson would know what to do. He tried to radio our company commander Captain Steele, who was just across the street huddled in the courtyard of a house. But the CO didn't answer. Watson tried to raise the Humvees from the Reaction Force, but he couldn't get them either. Time felt like it was collapsing on me. Every second felt like a huge waste of time. The life was bleeding out of Earl. I had to do something. Screw the radio and protocol. I yelled over to Captain Steele myself.

"Sir! I need a medevac now!"

He blew me off.

"We've got a head wound. I need to get him medevaced NOW!"

He gave me the hand. Captain Steele heard me but I'm pretty sure he had all kinds of other voices in his headset demanding his immediate attention as well. Finally he looked up and responded.

"Is he one of ours?" he wanted to know.

Is he one of ours? What? Are you kidding me? No, *he's a Somali*, I sarcastically mumbled to myself. But I knew what he meant.

"He's Delta," I said instead.

Captain Steele gave me the hand again, said something into the radio, and yelled back to me, "We don't know where the Humvees are. They can't find us."

What do you mean they can't find us? How can that be? We were only five blocks away from the target building. I just saw JB and Luman drive away a short while ago. They need to turn their butts around and come get us. How hard can this be?

But I had no idea how hard it actually was.

"If you're going through hell, keep moving."
(Winston Churchill)

Specialist Dominick Pilla was already dead when his body collapsed down into the cargo bay of the Humvee. Pilla was in the turret working the machine gun when a Somali gunman ran straight at them and fired a burst into Dominick's head.

The convoy had been trying to get the prisoners back to the airbase, but they ran into roadblock after roadblock and ambush after ambush. Now they were just trying to stay alive. A Humvee is a big target. Spray enough rounds at it or fire enough RPGs into it, and sooner or later you are going to start hitting the people inside. When Specialist Pilla went down, his squad leader in the front seat, Staff Sergeant Jeff Struecker, had a decision to make. Should he make the call now or wait to report that Task Force Ranger had just lost its first man.

The radios were on an open frequency so all elements could keep abreast of the others. Struecker knew it wasn't good for anyone listening in to hear someone was killed. "I knew it would take the wind out of their sails," he said. A KIA meant Task Force Ranger was no longer invincible, which is an erosion of confidence and an invitation for fear. And fear creates panic. Staff Sergeant Struecker had a job to do and that was to get the rest of his men out of there alive. To do that, he needed everyone focused. Struecker felt it would be best to wait to spread the word on Pilla's death. But his hand was forced when Sergeant First Class Bob Gallagher, the platoon sergeant of 3rd Platoon, radioed Struecker for a status report.

"How's it going?" asked Gallagher.

"Don't want to talk about it," replied Struecker still trying to stall the inevitable.

"Got any casualties?" asked Gallagher.

"Yeah. One."

"Who is he and what's his status?" It's a standard question anyone in charge would ask.

"It's Pilla."

"What's his status?" Gallagher pushed for more information.

Sergeant Struecker paused once more and thought about what to say. Gallagher backed him into a corner and Jeff wasn't going to lie to the man. So he answered.

"He's dead."

At that moment all radio traffic ceased. It's training right up until someone gets hit. When good men start going down around you, you are suddenly yanked into an entirely different level of reality. This was no movie set and these were not special effects going off around us. This was the cold hard truth. People were dying. No wonder Captain Steele was so preoccupied on his radio. Things were going from bad to worse and as far as he knew, he had just lost his first man as the man in charge. That couldn't have been an easy thing to hear. The burden of leadership is a heavy load to carry.

Dominick Pilla was a character. He had a thick Jersey accent and was constantly making people laugh. Everyone loved him. In our room he had a poster of G. Gordon Liddy and another of the Three Stooges. He had a collection of ball caps with old-school cartoon characters like Sylvester and Tweety Bird. Dominick was my roommate. He was my friend. I miss him.

"Delete any footage which includes the idea that war is not all together glamorous and noble."
(Joseph Breen, a Hollywood film association executive on what was acceptable to movie viewers)

Sergeant First Class Watson was still working on raising some-one who could help medevac Fillmore. I think he already knew they weren't going to send another helicopter in for us, because unbe-knownst to me, we had lost yet another aircraft. When Super 61 went down, Super 64 was called in to fill the gap. Within moments of coming into the flight pattern, 64 was hit by an RPG in the tail rotor, which quickly disintegrated and sent the aircraft into an uncontrolla-ble spin. Super 64 and the four men aboard crashed into a Mogadishu slum about a mile and half from where we were. Two MH-60s lay in heaps on the ground. The CSAR bird was out of action. No way they were risking another Black Hawk and crew to come get one man. We would have to find another way to evacuate Fillmore.

Sergeant Watson asked me if we could move the casualty out on foot. Maybe we could meet the Humvees somewhere nearby. But they weren't coming either. We had no idea the hell they were going through out there in the shooting gallery.

When the vehicles were redirected to turn around and come back to help us at the crash, things got even worse for them. An aircraft overhead was trying to guide them toward us. But the maze of alley-ways and the delay in communication was a breakdown that proved disastrous. By the time the guy giving directions could relay "take a right turn," it was too late. The lead elements of the convoy had already blown by. So they'd have to stop, back up and try again, going right back into the very same ambushes they had just escaped. The fact that there were now two crash sites only added to the confusion. Can you imagine how maddening and frustrating that must have felt to be on those trucks?

I ran back to the Delta team leader Sgt. First Class Norm Hooten who was still kneeling down next to Earl and called across the street, "Can we move him out on foot?"

He was very matter-of-fact in his answer, shaking his head as if to say it didn't matter.

"He's dead."

To this day, it still bothers me how little I felt at that moment compared to what you think you should feel as a Christian when someone dies in front of you. There was no overwhelming grief, remorse, or sadness like I would have imagined there should be. I felt guilty for not feeling sad. I also felt like a failure. We should have been able to do more. I was furious at Captain Steele for blowing me off. *Was he one of ours?* Weren't we all? I felt like I was supposed to know what to do in a situation like this. After all, I trained for years on what to do if you have a KIA. But something was wrong. That wasn't a KIA. It was Sergeant First Class Earl Fillmore, a good guy I knew personally who always took time to help out the younger Rangers. Someone I looked up to. We were exactly a month apart in age. He was from Pennsylvania, had a family, a wife, and more importantly, he was one of us. Earl was right there a minute ago. I know. I saw him. Now he's gone. And just like that, everything changed.

I never come to preach to any audience. But I will say this with absolute conviction to all who will hear my story; if you have never been a believer that there is a soul inside a human being, and that the soul goes someplace else when the body dies, then I am here to tell you that you are dead wrong. You've never been there when someone dies.

I don't know who that was or what it was. But it sure wasn't Earl Fillmore. He didn't look like he was playing dead in the movies. He didn't look like he was peacefully sleeping. He didn't look like him. What was there was a lifeless, empty suitcase made of flesh. I'd never been there when someone died before. But I can promise you with certainty there was no question in my mind Earl's soul was long gone from that body. I got a firsthand understanding of what Paul was talking about when he wrote to the church in Corinth about our heavenly dwelling outside the body.

> "Therefore, being always of good courage, and knowing that while we are at home in the body we are absent from the Lord—for we walk by faith, not by sight—we are of good courage, I say, and prefer rather to be absent from the body and at home with the Lord." (2 Cor. 5:6–8 NASB)

I also knew what my mission became. It was no longer about securing the crash site. The CSAR team and DiTomasso's squad would surely have that under control. It was no longer about trying to be a good squad leader and do all the right things. It was not about the country, the flag, or the greater glory of the Ranger Regiment. My sole purpose was clear—I was not going to let what just happened to Earl Fillmore happen to my three guys.

I glanced back at my men and there was Floyd, Suranski, and Dejesus, all three staring back across the street toward a dead SFC Fillmore. What do you think was going through young private Floyd's head when he saw the best of the best go down? A Delta operator, the super soldier he most looked up to, was just taken out. I know exactly what he was thinking.

When is it gonna be my turn?

"Courage is resistance to fear, mastery of fear, not the absence of fear." (Mark Twain)

That terrible screaming we heard a few minutes before is a pungent weapon for the enemy. It pierces your invincibility, knocks a hole in your armor, and lets fear begin to seep in. When good people start going down around you, the enemy steps up his attack and begins to lob fear in your direction. And fear is his most effective strategy against you.

You begin to feel that knot twist in your stomach. The backside of your brain is pumping all kinds of adrenaline into your body, all the while yelling at you to "SURVIVE! RUN AWAY! DON'T LET THAT HAPPEN TO YOU!"

The voice of survival can quickly turn to panic if you let it. Panic makes you forget your training. Panic makes you abandon the plan. Panic will choke you by the neck causing you to think only of yourself, and you will inevitably hang the people on your left and right out to dry.

It's OK to be afraid. Fear can be a great motivator as long as it is kept in check. As the person who leads the way, you must do everything in your power and use every available asset to defend your position and drive fear back. It is in these moments, the toughest of times and the darkest of nights, where we all must find something we call *character*.

Character is a lofty word. We put it up in our locker rooms. We hang it on posters in the office. We all want to be associated with people of character. We want our children to grow up into people of good character. We ourselves want to be known as a person of character. But what is it? Character is what God and the angels know of us and can best be described by the 6th stanza of the Ranger Creed:

Readily will I display the intestinal fortitude required to fight on to the Ranger objective and complete the mission. Though I be the lone survivor.

When fear begins to make its assault and tries to overrun your position, good leaders will find their strength of character. They will stand up in the face of adversity to provide purpose, direction, and motivation for those around them. They will push forward courageously, say "Follow me," and lead the way, even if the only person they are leading is themselves.

When I visit high schools around the country, I spend a great deal of time talking about the importance of strong character. This is what I tell them:

"I don't pretend to know how hard you have it or to know the challenges you face here at school or at home. I do know you will be faced with tough decisions. Character will get you through those hard times. But without a strong foundation of morals, values, and faith, your character will crumble. You've all seen it. You know those kids who made the wrong choices and paid the price.

"If you're not getting the foundation you need at home, then listen to your teachers and coaches. They will guide you in the right direction. If you aren't getting it here at school, then get it at church. If you don't go to church, then you better align yourself with people you know are of strong character. Emulate them. Do what they would do. Prepare yourself for the fight you will find yourself in. I can't tell you when and I can't tell you where. But I promise you it's coming. And if you have not done the hard work in advance, your character will crumble.

"Will you have what it takes to do the right thing and set an example for others to follow? Of course you will! I believe in you because you are here doing the hard work to better yourself. You understand that when you are called upon to do anything, you will only be as good as you prepared yourself to be. Train as you fight. Fight as you train. Lead by example."

History is jam-packed with stories about people of great character who saved the day with their leadership. The one common thread is always hard times and strong faith.

Moses trudged through the desert for forty years, but he found the strength of character to lead his people to the Promised Land, knowing he would never get to set foot in it.

David was a shepherd. He had no rank at all when he stepped into battle against the invincible Goliath. Outmanned and outarmed, the young shepherd took down the Philistine's best soldier with one rock and a whole lot of faith. David would grow into one of the greatest warrior kings Israel ever knew.

Esther put her life on the line when she went to the king and intervened on behalf of the Jewish people who were slated for extermination.

Job was a lesson in perseverance and faith.

Paul spent six years in prison, but still managed to stick to his ministry and lead the church despite the walls that bound him.

Floods. Famine. Storms. Earthquakes. Sickness. Persecution. Battles. Wars and death. God has used them all. Hard times are the cornerstone of character. But without a rock solid faith as the foundation, character will crumble.

As a unit, our character was built by countless hours of tough realistic training and overcoming difficulties as a team. We learned to have faith in each other, knowing without a doubt I had their backs and they had mine. Share enough hard times and you will soon find there is nothing you cannot endure and accomplish together.

"Character is best formed in the
stormy billows of the world." (Goethe)

Good men were going down. These weren't just any men. These were our friends and our comrades. All hell was breaking loose. The enemy was everywhere. Fear was doing its best to break us. It would have been very easy for any one of us to step out of the fight for just a moment. Hide behind a wall and act busy reloading or fidget with your gear. But to do that meant you were leaving the people around you hanging when they most needed you. So not a single one of my guys faltered. Not a single one flinched. I was so proud of them. I was inspired by them.

Let's take Suranski for instance, who just a short while before, during the movement from the target building, seemed like he was dangerously close to falling apart. He was standing up when he should have been taking cover. He wasn't making good decisions. But just like Floyd did earlier when he shot down a tree, Suranski had his moment when he found his character and became a Ranger who could lead the way.

Earlier in the fight, we were taking some intense fire at a critical intersection. There was a heavy weapon in a second-floor window of a building about a hundred yards down the road hammering our corner. No one could get across the street. Someone had to take that gun out. An M203 grenade launcher would be perfect. But that was going to be a tough shot.

"Suranski!"

"Roger, S'rgnt."

"There's a two-story building down the street on the right. It's got green shutters.

You see it?"

"Roger, S'rgnt."

"He's in the top window. Can you hit it?"

"Roger, S'rgnt."

Suranski took a quick peek around the corner. Believe me, it was quick. No one wanted to have their head out there for more than a blink, less you lose your head to a machine-gun-shooting clansman. Suranski identified the target, then pulled back behind the wall and chambered a grenade into the barrel of his 203.

The M203 looks like a big, fat shotgun-barrel mounted to the bottom of a rifle. You hand load a grenade shaped like a big, fat bullet down into the barrel. Charge it and then pull the trigger. With a loud *THUMP!* the grenade launches out of the tube. You can even watch the round as it arcs through the air to explode on impact at the place you aimed. It's almost like throwing a football. A quarterback gets so good at putting the ball exactly where he wants, he doesn't have to think about it.

So was the case with Suranski. I'm not even sure he leaned out around that wall for more than a second. But he thumped off a round that arced a hundred yards down the street, went straight through the second-story window with the green shutters, and *BAM*! He hit it!

"Good shot, Suranski!"

Private Eric Suranski found his character and lead by example at exactly the time we needed. His actions that day reflect great credit upon himself and the men who trained him.

I wanted to say something motivating and "leaderish" to my guys to get their minds off Earl Fillmore's death and back into the fight. Since I knew I couldn't be there to look after them, I reminded them one last time, "Floyd, look after Suranski. Suranski, look after Floyd. Listen to Dejesus. He's your team leader. He knows what he's doing. Take care of each other and we'll make it out of here. Hooah?"

The problem with my advice was by now the Roach was speaking Spanglish!

To me it sounded something like, "Weapon en la calle . . . por lo manos! Over there es un elephante en la cocina!"

"OK, so if you can understand what Dejesus is saying, do what he says. Otherwise, do what you know is right."

I didn't want to leave them on their own, but I had to. It must be the same sort of feeling parents get when they have to let their children go off on their own for the first time. Maybe they're heading off to college, getting married, or pulling out of the driveway with a brand new driver's license. Either way, you have to know in your heart you did everything you could to prepare them for the day when you could not be there at their side. How well your troops perform in the absence of your guidance says a great deal about you as a leader. Fortunately I was confident in their abilities to take care of each other. We trained our entire careers for a moment such as this. They would know what to do. They would find their character.

Dejesus hollered about someone with a weapon "en la calle el camino" or something. I turned to my 10 o'clock just in time to see a guy in a blue shirt about 150 meters away run out into the middle of the road.

"Weapon!"

I fired two rounds and the blue-shirted man went down out of view.

"You got 'em, S'rgnt."

It's amazing how steady a shot we became in these past months. The long, hot days shooting in the sand dunes paid off. Back at Fort Benning, I'm not sure I could have hit a moving target at that distance while spinning around on one knee.

There was another group of three or four armed men who ran across the same place and disappeared behind a big bush. I fired about three double shots into it, which probably didn't hit a thing.

Sergeant First Class Watson knew my rate of fire was undisciplined and already thinking ahead, wanted me to conserve ammunition. He reminded me to fire in controlled bursts and then tried to calm me down.

"Sergeant Thomas, take a deep breath. Calm down."

I knew he was right. But I was still so furious about the situation we were in and not being able to get Fillmore out. This is not the way it was supposed to be. We are the Rangers. That is Delta. We have the 160th up there. How is this possible? We gotta get out of here. What's taking so long? And then came the screaming.

"I'm hit! I'm hit!"

Shortly after insertion, Jim Lechner snapped the only photo taken during the battle. The target building is the tall one on the right. That's me running across the street toward my men against the wall. Mike Goodale is one of the guys kneeling behind the car wreck on the right.

Chapter 7

THE MEDIC AND THE MACHINE GUNNER AND OTHER ANGELS OF WAR

Surrender is not a Ranger word.
—5TH STANZA OF THE RANGER CREED

PRIVATE FIRST CLASS PETE NEATHERY believes in God. He told me so. He was our M60 machine gunner assigned to Chalk 3. He took up a position on the other side of the street, lying down behind a thin tin wall. No one told him to set up at that spot; he just knew it was a good position from which to cover all of us. He was firing his gun back toward the left-turn intersection when he was shot in the arm. His scream pierced the air.

★ 119 ★

Specialist Richard Strous was our medic. We called him Doc, which I always thought was a good name for a medic. He was shot up and blown up. Literally. While running across a street a round hit one of Doc's smoke grenades and like David Copperfield, he instantly disappeared in a cloud of white. In the confusion, Sergeant First Class Watson yelled to Floyd, who was the closest one to Doc at the time.

"FLOYD! Where is Strous?"

A clearly upset and slightly bewildered Floyd yelled back, "He blew up, Sergeant! He blew up!"

Doc, of course, in perfect comedic timing, immediately stepped out of the smoke, looking like a cartoon character who just fell for the old exploding-smoke-grenade gag. His face was caked with white dust. The cloth edges around his helmet were sticking straight up. And to add insult, his britches were blown out at the crotch. But apparently, you don't need your pants to save a life.

As soon as I heard Neathery scream, "I'm hit!" I took off to help. It was an automatic reaction. I probably should have stayed with my guys, but they knew what they were doing and were in good shape—a lot better than Neathery, it would seem. I sprinted across the road running directly toward Captain Steele and just about stepped on him. I jumped over Lieutenant Lechner, our executive officer, kicked down a small metal wall in the way, and came out on the other side of it to a startled Mike Kurth and Private Erico. Another ten yards and I was there. It probably took me all of thirty seconds.

In less time than it takes to reheat a cup of coffee in the microwave, Doc had already dragged Neathery out of the street, cut open his shirtsleeve to access the wound, shoved Kerlix gauze into the hole to stop the bleeding, and was busy starting an IV to replace lost fluids and deter shock. Doc was going about his business just as calmly as if he was teaching a class back in the comfort and safety of the barracks.

To see Doc pull Neathery from the line of fire, you would think he was simply annoyed that someone was trying to shoot at him. God loves medics. They are His angels of war. Had there been water there, I'm sure Doc would have walked across it. Doc rolled over to Neathery's side as if he'd done it a hundred times and with one arm pulled him back behind a wall.

Doc was certainly not the fastest, most physical Ranger in the platoon. Unless you were sick or he was teaching a class on combat life saving, we didn't see Doc all that much. He mostly kept to himself. In fact, he was kinda weird, as most medics are. It's a peculiar person who enjoys all that trauma. In Doc's defense, I think his oddness may have been due to his unlimited access to the medications! He may have been a little nuts, but Doc always had his nose in a book. He was always looking for a better way to save a life. He did not get complacent and offer excuses saying, "I've done every-thing I need to do. I've met the standards." No, Doc was constantly trying to improve himself and those around him because in his mind, good was not good enough when better was expected.

He had only been in the Army a couple years and was younger than a college graduate. But when it came to saving lives, Richard Strous was an absolute pro. Why? Because Doc knew he was the one piece of the puzzle that made everything work. The entire well-being of our platoon hinged on him and his ability to do his job. In the unlikely event he was ever needed, lives were surely on the line and squarely in his hands. If Specialist Strous couldn't save a life, who could?

The bullet impacted Neathery in the right arm. It traveled up the bone and exited near the shoulder, basically disconnecting the muscle like a knife fillets a fish. Doc was already starting to administer the pain meds.

"Is it bad? Is it bad?" Neathery wanted to know but he didn't want to look.

It looked to me like someone tried to cut off his bicep.

"Uh, it's pretty gross man."

Doc jumped in like a mother lying about how good her daughter's new braces look.

"Noooo, it's fine, Pete. It's nothing. Everything is OK. You're gonna be just fine." Strous shot me a look as if to say, "You seriously need to work on your bedside manner."

Neathery seemed to be handling it remarkably well. He even kept his sense of humor.

"Sergeant, I hope they send me home for this!"

You know when you go to a class or a meeting and the instructor or speaker encourages the audience to ask questions? They usually say something like, "Feel free to ask questions. Remember, there is no such thing as a stupid question." I beg to differ. There are stupid questions and I asked one.

"Hey Pete, does that hurt?"

"Yeah, it hurts! But I'm OK though," he reassured me.

Funny. He was reassuring me. Sure seemed like it should have been the other way around. As I moved away from Neathery to get behind the gun, he grabbed me by the pant leg and added one more thing: "Hey S'rgnt Thomas, I want you to know I believe in God." I wished I'd had a better follow-up for Pete, but all I could think to say was, "Well, He believes in you too, my man." I smiled and patted him on his good arm. As I moved away to get that M-60 back in action I thought to myself, I sure hope He believes in all of us right now. Because we're gonna need all the help we can get.

"There are no atheists in foxholes."
(from the field sermon given to the troops by
William Thomas Cummings in Battan 1942)

A couple of months later, I would go visit Neathery at Walter Reed Hospital. His arm was healing up well so I didn't feel bad about giving him a hard time.

"Hey Pete, you remember when you got shot back there in Mogadishu?"

"Uh, yeah, I remember, S'rgt," as he showed me the erector set holding his arm together.

"Yeah, well what I want to know is how come we had to carry you off the street? You were shot in the arm."

We joked for a while as we walked down to the hospital cafeteria. Over some ice cream and coffee, Pete thanked me for that moment on the street. The pat on the "good arm" and the kind word meant a great deal to him at the time. It was such a small thing in a big, chaotic world. But you never know how far a simple act of kindness can mean to someone.

"Through humor, you can soften some of the worst blows that life delivers. And once you find laughter, no matter how painful your situation might be, you can survive it." (Bill Cosby)

I first met Leroy during a Memorial Day event at the Coca-Cola corporate headquarters in Atlanta. The executives at Coke invited me to come sing a couple patriotic songs and tell the story of Task Force Ranger. It was a proud and humbling moment considering veterans like Leroy were in attendance. To tell you the truth, I felt a bit intimidated. What could I possibly say that most of those old guys hadn't already seen tenfold?

I noticed Leroy as I walked out of the auditorium after the event. He was standing off to the side by himself. Something moved me to go over and say hello. I simply wanted to shake his hand and thank him for his service to our nation. I thought that would be a kind thing to do. I quickly realized it was me who would find the blessing in our meeting.

"Young man," he said, "I'm glad you went out of your way to say hello because I wanted to say something to you, but I didn't want to impose."

With the irreplaceable wisdom of a man who had been there and done that, Leroy told me what God wanted me to hear. "You didn't make it out of that battle because the Somalis were bad shots. You made it out because God has a plan for you and you have a responsibility. You have a gift, young man. You can sing a song. You can tell a story. If you don't, then who will?"

He then went on to talk about the parable of the talents Jesus tells in the book of Matthew. Basically the lesson is about the gifts we are given by God. It is up to us to use them wisely. Use them for purpose, direction, and motivation. If you bury your talents and are afraid to use them, then you are throwing away God's gifts. Take what God has given you, use them or lose them.

"For everyone who has will be given more, and he will have an abundance. Whoever does not have, even what he has will be taken from him." (Matthew 25:29)

Just like that, everything changed for me. Honestly, I always felt a bit guilty about being paid for the speaking events. Like a powerful propaganda machine, the enemy within me was convincing me I was unworthy and did not deserve this attention, that I was wrong for "taking advantage" of the situation. The twisted truth I was willing to believe may as well have been played over a prison camp loudspeaker over and over: "You are lucky to be here. You are using the memory of your dead comrades as a platform for your career. How do you think they would feel if they were here? But they can't be here because they are dead and you are not."

Like a prison wall I built all around myself, the fear of success and the guilt of survival held me back and kept me from fully being where God was leading. I needed help breaking out. And there it was. Standing in the halls of the Coca-Cola Corporation in downtown Atlanta.

Leroy was a P-51 mustang pilot during WWII. When you talk to Leroy, he will tell you the most difficult thing he ever faced as an airman was not the intense dog fights with Nazi aircraft over the skies of Germany. Nor was it the punishing anti-aircraft fire that was always a given when escorting the big bombers to their targets deep into enemy territory. It wasn't the two fiery plane crashes he somehow managed to survive about which he told me, "I was sure I was going to die because the plane was upside down. But I walked away without a scratch." If you ask Leroy what the hardest part about that war was, his answer is quick and without hesitation.

It was the racism and segregation by the very same country he was fighting for . . . Leroy was one of the legendary Tuskegee Airmen. They were an all-black fighter squadron that distinguished themselves with gallantry over the skies of Europe, fighting the Germans as bomber escorts for our Air Corp. Many of his comrades did not come home, laying down their lives for an American dream they knew they could not share.

Leroy wanted to be an airline pilot after the war. No one would hire him because he was "colored." He instead became an instructor, training pilots for the very job he could not have. Despite it all, Leroy is happy, kind, and caring. Nowadays his business card lists him as a Grandfather, a Writer-Lecturer-Yardman-Optimist-Dreamer.

Of course it probably seems fitting that two warriors from battles past would meet at a Veteran's Day event. But you may think it a bit serendipitous or ironic that two relentless dreamers could connect through the commonality of something terrible like combat. However, I believe there are no coincidences when it comes to meeting those who touch our lives.

It began as an ordinary act of kindness, a small gesture of gratitude, a simple thank-you. Though Leroy and I talked only briefly the day we met, the impact of that moment helped changed the course of my life. God had something to say to me I needed to hear. He found a way to tell me through the voice of an eighty-year-old black man. "You have been given a gift. Use it. For if you don't tell their story, who will?"

> "Do not forget to entertain strangers,
> for by so doing some people have entertained
> angels without knowing it." (Hebrews 13:2)

Sergeant First Class Watson wanted to know the situation with Neathery. He was across the street giving me a full-body mime impersonation of someone quickly losing their patience with my lack of information dissemination. His arms were open wide as if to say, "WELL??? Are you going to tell me what's going on over there or not?"

Doc knew he was going to need more fluids, but they were in his bigger aid bag across the street at Watson's position.

"We need Doc's aid bag," I screamed over the noise.

"Hold on. We'll get it over to you," came his reply.

I quickly interjected. "I can come get it."

"No! Wait right there," Watson repeated.

In hindsight, it's easy to see why SFC Watson wanted me to wait. He was trying to motivate another soldier to get into the fight and start stepping up. Sergeant Hulst came to us from a different unit. He was a nice enough guy, just never really fit in with our group because he was a transplant and hadn't grown up in the Ranger battalion.

I remember Hulst always wore those silly over-the-top hooah-hooah killing man T-shirts; they had drawings on them of superhero Rangers carrying around eighty-three different weapons. He talked real tough. I guess he felt like he had something to prove. But Sergeant Hulst earned his Ranger tab and he was a squad leader. So you had to respect the man. I'll tell you though, he was lucky to have Sergeant Randy Ramaglia as his team leader. Randy was the glue that held that squad together.

Sergeant Hulst got the assignment to bring the aid bag across the street. By now it seemed to me the street was the killing zone. Rounds were still coming and going at a torrential pace. Understandably no one wanted to move from the safety of their positions unless it was absolutely necessary. Somehow I didn't mind the vulnerability of the street. Just the act of running and moving made me feel more secure. It would have only taken me a few seconds to sprint over and sprint back. But Hulst had another technique in mind.

He began to low-crawl through the sandy street pushing the aid bag in front of him. I thought he was nuts. Speed is security. Move and move fast. I almost laughed at how ridiculous it looked. Randy was thinking the same thing because he saw me and just rolled his eyes.

But there is something to be said for slow and steady. Hulst managed to successfully get the bag halfway across the street to where Specialist John Collett set up a machine gun position in a slight defilade in the road. The tortoise never stopped. He just pushed the bag at Collett and pulled a low-crawl U-turn, heading back from where he came.

Wow, I thought. *That's a technique. Good job Hulst. OK my turn.*

"Collett! Cover me. On three. Ready?"

"Roger, Sergeant. I gotcha."

"One . . . two . . . three!"

Collett let loose a long burst with his SAW machine gun and I sprinted out to meet him. Pete Rose would have been proud of my face-first slide, and the umpire most assuredly would have called me "SAFE!" I made some kind of a smart-aleck comment to Collett like, "Isn't this fun?" and grabbed the aid bag, and darted back to Doc.

The guys who shot Neathery were still there and our heaviest casualty-producing weapon, the M60, was sitting idle. So I jumped down behind it, pulled back the charging handle, and got it ready to fire. Erico was helping to guide me.

"He's behind the wall, Sergeant."

About fifty yards away, back toward the left-turn intersection, was a little three-foot concrete wall. And sure enough, up popped a head. Then an AK-47. The guy wasn't really aiming; he was just gonna spray it.

I fired up the top of the wall hoping that maybe I had gotten him or, at the very least, that it would keep his head down. I didn't get him.

I saw movement again. I fired. *DAT DAT DAT DAT DAT DAT . . . DAT DAT DAT . . . click click click.* I was out of rounds.

A machine gun without rounds is about as useful as a wet match. It isn't exactly gonna set the woods on fire. If you ever get into a discussion with someone about gun control, you tell them Keni said, "Guns are not the issue. Ammo is the problem."

I had a fully automatic, gas-operated, high-powered machine gun I could do absolutely nothing with. Like a car needs fuel, a gun needs bullets to operate. The rest of the 7.62 belts were in Neathery's butt pack, on which he was lying. It didn't look like he was going to jump up and bring them to me because, by now, he had IV tubes coming out of his body and was half-loopy from the pain killers. We'd have to cut it off him and that would mean more time I didn't feel we had.

In the meantime, I was out in the street with a useless machine gun and no rifle. I left it with Doc Strous thinking he might need it. I did have a shotgun Velcroed to my leg, but at this range all it would do is maybe make a loud bang and scare the bad guys. And at that point, we were way past scaring people. So I did the next best thing. I pulled out a grenade.

"I'm gonna frag it. Collett, cover me!"

In basic training you are taught how to throw a grenade. Like anything in the Army, there is a step-by-step procedure.

Step one: Pull the pin.

Step two: Take aim. The instructors had you stand up, point to the target with one arm, and lean back to throw with the other. You looked exactly like that little plastic green army man. Wouldn't you know it, that's not exactly what I did. I popped up from the ground and assumed the ridiculous position. If there was a Heisman Trophy for grenade-throwing, they would have modeled it after me.

Step three: Throw the grenade. When you let go of the baseball sized mini-bomb, this releases the spoon and engages the five-second fuse. What instructors don't take into account during training is the superhuman strength you obtain from the adrenaline overdose pumped into your body during a life and death situation, such as the one we were in. I put that grenade so far over the wall it blew up on the porch of a house well past my intended target.

"You missed," Erico informed me.

"Yeah, thanks."

I let loose of my other grenade, but his time I threw it straight at the wall like a catcher going to second base. I don't know how I did it, but I put it in exactly the same place as before.

"You missed," Erico informed me again like a backseat-driving mom who's driving the driver crazy.

"Yes, I can see that" I wanted to say. "Thank you, Captain Obvious."

I couldn't hit water if I was standing in a boat. I clearly needed a lot more practice throwing grenades. At least my shot group was tight. Floyd would later tell me he saw guys moving in the porch where the grenades landed. He thought that's where I was aiming. Lucky shot.

So the shooters were still there shooting and I was still out in the street with an empty M-60, no rifle, a nonapplicable shotgun, no grenades, and a partridge in a pear tree. I yelled to my buddy Sergeant Randy Ramaglia, "Hey, Ramaglia, I'm out of grenades. Toss me your grenades!"

He looked at me like I had a clown nose on and a big red afro coming out of my helmet. It wasn't that Randy didn't want to give me his grenades. It was that he was well aware of something I seemed to have overlooked, which was throwing grenades at each other was a bad idea! High margin of error there. At no time in our training had we ever tossed explosive devices at one another like they do in the movies. Now was not the time to start winging it. Train as you fight. Fight as you train.

By now you've probably figured out what I still had not and what Sergeant Watson was trying so hard to tell me. He was pointing at his back in convulsions. *What's wrong with him?* I thought. *What's he saying?* I couldn't tell.

Then I saw his lips moving slowly and deliberately. This time I heard Sean T. Watson, loud and clear, because he was using that parental tone of voice again. You know the one, the one that gets things done.

"USE THE LAW! THE LAW . . . . ON YOUR BACK!"

Oh yeah! I had been carrying a 4.5-pound rocket launcher around for so long I forgot it was there! Sergeant Watson's words from months earlier were now reverberating in my head like a Jewish mother's I-told-you-so. "Better to have and not need than to need and not have." Excellent combat advice.

The drill sergeants of basic training would have been very proud of me because I did everything just like they taught me. The LAW (light anti-tank weapon) comes with written instructions printed on the side. My favorite line reads, *This side toward enemy.* You have to be at least 10 percent smarter than the equipment so they make it real simple for you. I extended the tube, slapped open the sights, took aim, and even remembered to turn around to Erico and Kurth and give the proper warning, "Back blast area clear!"

I pushed in the detent button and winced as the shock of the noise hammered my skull. The launcher jerked, then suddenly got lighter as the rocket cleared the tube. I followed the thin smoke trail as it hurtled toward the target and impacted exactly where I aimed. *BAMMM!* The LAW didn't miss. There was now a two-foot hole in the wall where a bad guy used to be.

Seemed easy. But I will tell you, had we not had the opportunity to fire a real LAW just weeks before in the sand dunes, I never would have hit the target when it needed to be hit. They fire differently than you think they will. In basic training we never had a real rocket; we only learned the procedure. But Task Force Ranger made certain the resources were available to ensure everyone knew what it felt like to fire a live LAW. Train as you fight. Fight as you train.

Resources is an important word when it comes to training and preparing for your mission. Sometimes, though, you are not provided with everything you would have wanted or thought you needed to accomplish the task at hand. That is unfortunate. But the job must be done never the less. So you are forced to improvise. You make do and you surprise those around you with your solutions and creativity.

I get the opportunity to speak to a lot of teachers and educators at professional development conferences around the nation. Most of the districts I talk to are not the wealthy white-bred upper middle class school systems so well-funded by local taxes and a community with money to spare.

I get invited to the rural areas of California, West Texas, and South Florida—the way-out-there counties and challenged areas who depend entirely on grossly under-funded state budgets to accomplish the monumental task of educating our nation's youth. Places where English as a second language is a main concern. Where community involvement is hard to come by because a large majority of the parents don't speak English and will be moving away next year in search of work wherever they can find it. These are school systems where the challenges are great and the resources are small.

But teachers and educators are a resourceful and passionate bunch who believe in their purpose and will do what they must to accomplish their mission. So they go to Target and they buy pencils and copy machine paper with their own money. They reuse outdated, torn and tattered textbooks for years until the books literally fall apart. They spend their days off to travel to professional development conferences to share ideas and better themselves.

Yes, they deserve more training, more books, more money, and more resources. But the sad reality is they sometimes don't have everything they need or would like to have. So they continue to find ways to lead those kids and provide the necessary purpose, direction, motivation, and inspiration. They continue to set an example for others to follow when most others would have quit. Why? Because someone is counting on them to do so.

If you happen to be someone in charge who makes budgetary decisions and are tasked with allocating resources to various job-training opportunities, remember this: You may have the greatest soldiers in the world working for you who will use every last ounce of effort they have to complete the mission you give them. But they will only be as good as the training you provide allows them to be. As good as they are, they can be even better. Give them that opportunity. You train as you fight so that you will fight as your train.

"The object of war is to survive it." (John Irving)

I barely had time to congratulate myself on the well-placed rocket shot when there it was again—the screaming. B company's second in command and executive officer First Lieutenant Jim Lechner had been shot. I busted back through the same tin wall I had kicked in earlier and got there just in time to see the Delta medic Bart Bullock dragging Lechner inside the house and Captain Steele low-crawling inside.

The next time I would see Jim Lechner was many years later while on a USO tour to Iraq. He gave me a big hug as I stepped off the aircraft at Camp Ramadi. He had been promoted quite a bit since the last time we'd both been in a combat zone together. He was now wearing the oak leaves of a Lieutenant Colonel and I was wearing a USO ball cap with a guitar slung across my back. I was part of the Sergeant Major of the Army Kenneth Preston's Holiday USO Tour. This was one of our daily visits to meet and greet with the men and women stationed throughout Iraq. Lieutenant Colonel Lechner was a battalion commander for the 1st Armored Division "Old Ironsides" and was doing amazing things there in Ramadi.

If you remember the stories in the news, Ramadi was a hotbed for insurgents and al-Qaeda. It was a highly unstable and definitely unsafe place to be. At the time, American troops were training an Iraqi police force in Ramadi, but in its infantile state was corrupt and incompetent. If insurgents were going to be rooted out, it was going to take a stronger local effort.

Lieutenant Colonel Lechner had the foresight and the humility to bring together all the sheiks and ask for their help. Each tribe leader had a substantial force of armed followers. If you brought them all to the table and made it worth their while, together they would have the capabilities to clean the city up and break the terroristic stronghold. It would take a united and coordinated effort to make the streets safe again for all its citizens.

With Lechner's guidance and a whole lot of support, that's exactly what happened. There was a photo that ran later in the *USA Today* of a smiling Jim Lechner without his body armor playing checkers outside a shop in downtown Ramadi. It was a symbolic gesture to show the public that the streets were safe again and progress was being made.

It was so good to see Jim again. It had been a long time. We talked while I signed autographs, and then I sang a few songs for the troops there in the chow hall. He looked great. You couldn't even notice the limp. Hard to believe because the 7.62 round that found him on a Mogadishu street thirteen years earlier had shattered his tibia in a gazillion places. Back then, no one thought that young Lieutenant Lechner would ever walk again, much less stay in the Army and make history as a battalion commander over a decade later in another war in Iraq.

The limp was gone but there was one very conspicuous possession that Jim Lechner still had with him from that fight in the streets of Mogadishu. On the right shoulder of his uniform was the 3rd Ranger Battalion scroll. He still wore it proudly. As a soldier, if you've ever been part of a combat operation, you get to wear your unit's insignia on the right shoulder of your uniform for the remainder of your military career, no matter what unit you may be assigned to. It instills pride and lets the world know who your band of brothers are. If throughout your career, you are deployed to a war zone with multiple units, as Jim had been, then you are allowed to choose which unit you will display as your combat patch. Men who have earned the right to wear a combat Ranger Battalion scroll on their right arm will seldom choose another.

"The battles that count aren't the ones for gold medals. The struggles within yourself— the invisible, inevitable battles inside all of us—that's where it's at." (Jesse Owens)

The screaming was immediate and high-pitched as Lt. Lechner wailed out in obvious pain. He was part of our command element with Captain Steele. When Jim was hit, both men were lying on the ground outside of the building just behind me, still in the same place where I had jumped over them in my sprint to help Neathery. They had stayed in the same spot too long. If enough rounds are fired at an area, sooner or later those rounds are going to hit something or someone. That something was Jim's leg.

The terrible distress in a comrade's voice is almost always answered immediately by a buddy who comes running to help as a couple of us did. But initially, rounds were impacting all around, so Captain Steele's first reaction was to roll out of the line of fire. Bart Bullock, the Delta medic, responded as any medic would, without hesitation, and sprinted out from cover to help the wounded man.

A lot was made of that moment later on. Some of the operators felt Captain Steele's actions were less than exemplary and that they would have done things differently had they been in Mike Steele's shoes. But that's just it. They weren't in his shoes and I've always felt those accusations were unwarranted. But then again, you have to take into account that those guys pointing fingers weren't too fond of Mike Steele and his regimented, hard-nosed personality.

He had been a Georgia Bulldog down lineman under Vince Dooley. What did you expect? We called him Coach. I liked Captain Steele. I had gone to the University of Florida and grew up a Gator. So we had a healthy rivalry where we could talk about things other than Rangering. I suppose I got to talk to the CO more than most young sergeants would chitchat with their company commander.

One day our squad had the opportunity to do some high-speed room-clearing training with the Delta boys. They taught us their techniques for clearing a building and how we could improve upon the basic close quarters battle drills we were taught in the Ranger Regiment. Afterwards Captain Steele and I were talking. He wanted to know what I thought of the training and their methods. I told him I felt like it was a better technique and flowed a lot more smoothly. He listened and nodded as I talked through some of the exercises the D-boys had taught us.

"You know, Sgt. Thomas, it's not that I don't respect how good they are at what they do. I get that. But what you have to understand is these men are seasoned NCOs with years of experience. You know why our training has to stay so basic? It's because we have privates who are new and inexperienced soldiers coming into the regiment. It's our job to get them up to combat speed quickly and efficiently. We have to keep it simple."

I understood his logic and why he tried so hard to keep us separated as units. He knew we looked up to the Delta operators. They were the varsity squad. They were big brother. A young Ranger might be tempted into thinking he could ignore his Ranger training and instead do what Delta does. This could prove disastrous and was unacceptable. It's not that Mike Steele disliked the men of Delta or believed them to be "undisciplined cowboys" as the movie portrayed. Quite the opposite. He respected their level of training and expertise. But their methods were not our methods. For command and control purposes, he could not afford to mix the two. Because he tried so hard to keep the integrity of B company separated from the Delta squadron, Captain Steele rubbed a lot of the operators the wrong way. As a result there was a noticeable tension between our command and theirs.

The allegations, after the fact, made by those Delta men bothered Mike Steele for a long time. Months later, when we were back at Fort Benning returning to life in battalion, he called me into his office. An investigation was underway, and I could see he felt humiliated that anyone could think him capable of cowardice.

"Sergeant Thomas, you were there. What did you think?" I have to admit it felt a little awkward, a captain asking a sergeant for reassurance. But this was not a conversation between ranks. It was two men who respected each other. You know what I told him?

"Sir, it looked to me like you did everything anyone could have expected. Whether or not you could have done more, well that's for you to decide. Only you know what you see when you look down the sights of your rifle, and what you do about it is a choice you have to live with."

He shook my hand and thanked me with a simple "hooah." It was sincere. Mike Steele was never the most eloquent man. He was a Georgia Bulldog for crying out loud. But he was a strong Christian and a man of honor. I believe he should be at peace with his actions, at that point in the battle.

The burden of leadership quite often makes you a target and will throw you into the line of fire. You can be certain others are going to judge you, your actions, and the choices you make. Small wonder most folks are hesitant to take a stand and lead the way. Who wants to set themselves up for that kind of scrutiny?

In His famous Sermon on the Mount, Jesus gives us the Beatitudes. At first glance, they look like a simple pronouncement of blessings for all God's children to include the poor, the meek, and the pure at heart. But this Scripture is more than just a list of recipients. Think of it as a block of instruction given the same way the military trains people up to greatness. It's a tried and true method of gradual learning called Crawl, Walk, Run. Keep the task simple at first then build up the skill set until you are an absolute expert with the task at hand.

All algebra starts with fractions and multiplication. All calculus starts with an expert understanding of algebra. All differential equations require an uncommon knowledge of calculus. Crawl. Walk. Run.

So look at the Beatitudes as a step-up process where each blessing is a rung in the ladder helping us in our climb to become leaders of men for the army of God. It starts at the very bottom. "Blessed are the poor in spirit." We all start broken. But God is there for us to mend us, to fix us, to make us better than we were. As we grow in our relationship with Him, more is expected of us. Blessed are the merciful. Blessed are the pure in heart. Blessed are the peacemakers. We keep climbing the ladder until it culminates at the highest step looking back down from a cross. "Blessed are you when they revile and persecute you, and say all kinds of evil against you" (Matt. 5:11 NKJV). When you get to the top, they are going to try and knock you down.

When you become a leader for Christ, for your community, for your friends, family, and coworkers, you have to know going in that it's not going to be an easy gig. People are going to judge you. They will criticize you and point a finger, stating what you "should have done" in accordance with how *they* think things should have been done. Take the lead on a group project and you watch. Someone is not going to be happy with your direction. At the very least, you will be the Monday morning topic of the office armchair quarterbacks who were too afraid of failure to raise their hands in the first place. So they'll sit back and hide behind a know-it-all front, cloaking their lack of self-confidence by lashing out at you. And they'll do it behind your back, because confronting you face-to-face would require the very self-confidence that failed them in the first place. The greater the cause, the higher the stakes, and the more the opposition will despise you. At worst, they'll arrest you, beat you with whips and chains, drive nails through your hands, and hang you out to die.

There will come a day when you will be in charge, courageously doing what you think is right, and you will take a beating for it. When that day comes, I want you to remember what Doc Strous correctly said to reassure Pete Neathery who was lying there in the dirt with a gaping hole in his arm, bleeding in the streets of a third-world country way too far from home.

"It's nothing, Pete. Everything is OK. You're gonna be just fine."

Then I want you to pull out your Bible, read Matthew chapter 5, verses 11 and 12 and know you are in great company.

> "Blessed are you when they revile and persecute you, and say all kinds of evil against you falsely for My sake. Rejoice and be exceedingly glad, for great is your reward in heaven, for so they persecuted the prophets who were before you." (NKJV)

You are going to get knocked down. You are going to take a hit. Do not let that discourage you. Heal up. Learn from it and get back in the fight. There is someone to your left and right counting on you.

Doc Richard Strous, Eric Suranski, me, and David Floyd.

Chapter 8

THE LONG NIGHT

I will never leave a fallen comrade to fall into the hands of the enemy.
—5TH STANZA OF THE RANGER CREED

"EVERYONE COME. LET US KILL the Americans. Kill the Rangers. Kill them all!"

Mosques around the city were calling for evening prayers and I could only imagine what those foreign voices were saying over the loud speakers. We were a long way from home. Man, how did we get here? What day was it? It felt like a week ago I was enjoying the sun writing a letter to my mom. But the sun was gone, giving way to the shifting shadows of twilight.

What should have been an hour-long mission was now looking like it would last a lifetime. Which, for some of us, we feared might not be as long as the immortality of our youth once believed.

The number of men going down was starting to outpace the rest of us. Erico was Chalk 3's latest. He got hit in the arm when he took over the machine gun for me. Lieutenant Larry Perino reported his Chalk 1 had so many casualties; they were officially "combat ineffective." If we stayed out in the streets, eventually there would be too many casualties to effectively evacuate without proper transport. It was time to move inside.

The plan was to consolidate the wounded by bringing them into a casualty collection point (CCP). For our platoon we decided it would be the house I was positioned by and shooting from all day. It was the same one where Lechner was shot. It also became the de-facto command center since both Captain Steele and the Delta commander set up shop inside.

Never mind the family was still in there. War is hell. We did everything we could to ensure their safety. We put the mother and her very frightened children in the back room behind mattresses, just in case their fellow countrymen should decide to start launching RPG rockets through the stucco walls. Suranski helped me move Erico and Neathery inside to one of the rooms, and then I went back out with Dejesus to help guide the rest of the platoon in.

Ambient light was fading fast. It would be hard to see soon. One by one, the rest of the men in Chalk 3 moved off the street and came to my position. Dejesus pulled security as I pointed them to the door opening until all the platoon was safely inside. Sergeant Randy Ramaglia was one of the last men to get there. By what was left of the light, I could see he was still managing a smile.

"And you will be called Pinto. Why Pinto?
Why not?" (from the movie *Animal House*)

Randy Ramaglia loved raisin bread. It was always a part of his delicious and nutritious breakfast. The type of cereal you got to eat was mostly determined by when you arrived at the chow hall. If you got there early enough, you might score a box of Froot Loops or granola. But most of the time, all that was ever left was the crappy ones like Corn Flakes and Raisin Bran. Never seemed to bother Randy, though. He was always happy as long as he had some raisin bread to go with it.

When sung to the tune of "Mustang Sally," "Raisin Bread Randy" sings very well. I don't pretend to know how my mind works at times or why I started singing "Raisin Bread Randy" to the tune of "Mustang Sally" one morning, but it sounded catchy and it stuck. So it became my nickname for the guy.

I, too, had a favorite food. It was the terrible defrost-and-serve cornbread we got every once in a while on steak night or, as our cook Private Moorecock once called it, "A close relative to the cow." Since no one else liked the frozen cornbread and I didn't eat cow or whatever its close relative was, people would take the meat and trade me the bread. Pretty soon, I was getting pelted with it. "Here ya go, Cornbread." The name hung around like a bad country song.

"What up, Cornbread?" Ramaglia joked as he clunked down next to Dejesus and me outside the CCP.

"Nothing much, Raisin Bread Randy. Man," I told him, "you're doing a damn good job over there with your squad. I heard you out there motivating your people. They're lucky to have you!"

"Naw brother, you're the one who's doing good. Running around in the streets all crazy-like!"

I hadn't really thought about it, but Randy was right. I'd been moving a lot and I was tired. It had been a crazy day but I knew it wasn't over yet. Just because you can't see the enemy, doesn't mean he isn't there. But you know, I wasn't really scared. I had the Roach with me and my main man Randy Ramaglia. We were the three amigos and together we were invincible.

We stayed out there in silence peering into the shadows as darkness fell on the streets of dirty Mogadishu like a hammer on an anvil. It was gonna be a long night.

"[I] shall not be afraid of the terror by night,
nor of the arrow that flies by day
for the Lord my God is on my side."
(Psalm 91:5, author paraphrase)

It was frustrating. The three of us could hear the bad guys moving into the positions we had just occupied less than twenty minutes ago. It sure would have been an opportune time to have my night vision mounted on my weapon. Night Optical Devices (NODs) would have evened the playing field real quick. We could have taken down every one of those shadow men creeping around out there in the dark.

Don't forget nothin'! I could hear Captain Rogers yelling his I-told-you-so's from the grave. It is better to have and not need, than to need and not have—a lesson I had now learned twice that day. We are constantly relearning what those before us have tried so hard to teach us.

But NODs or no NODs, this sitting around in a defensive perimeter licking our wounds was not at all Ranger-like. We were supposed to be the aggressors. We were the storm troopers. We were the 75th Ranger Regiment for crying out loud. We were the best infantry soldiers in the world. Here we were feeling all rode hard and put up wet, waiting for some third-world thugs to come and get us.

I strained my ears listening for the shuffling of feet or the clinking of a weapon, anything that would give me a fix on where the enemy might be lurking. Best I could tell, there were a handful of guys about a hundred yards away and slowly closing in. I wondered if maybe we could circle around behind them. You know, like how we used to do as kids when we played Army back in the neighborhood. There was a problem with that plan though. This wasn't our neighborhood. We didn't know the streets like they did. But we needed to do something. The enemy was getting too close. Since Randy and I were made from the same mold, I didn't have to say a word to him. He was already thinking the same thing. It was time to go on the offensive.

"Roach," I whispered. "We're moving!"

Dejesus must have thought I meant back inside because that was the direction he started to move. You would think I'd have known better than to believe we could run off into the dark and save the day. I didn't. But God did. Because that's right about when He showed up ensuring we should stay right where we were.

God appears to man in many shapes and forms throughout the Bible, especially in the Old Testament. One of his favorite tools to make a point was fire. He was a blazing bush when He gave Moses his first warning order. The Lord rained down fire and brimstone when He torched the cities of Sodom and Gomorrah. In the book of Job "the fire of God" falls from heaven and burns up all of Job's sheep and all the shepherds.

In the book of Keni, God showed up in the shape of an AH-6 attack helicopter reaping death and pouring fire from the sky above. The air erupted directly over our heads as two Little Birds opened up with their mini-guns one after the other. At 4,000 rounds a minute, the expended brass casings were raining down around us like hot hail from hell. The lightning effect of the guns lit up the street just long enough for us to see at least a dozen Somalis who were a whole lot stronger in numbers and a whole lot closer than I thought.

The pilots fired everything they had. As the Somalis ran to pull their wounded and dead from the streets, one of the birds banked around again. Out of ammunition, the pilot did what he could to hold the enemy back by buzzing their heads. Randy caught a glimpse of the shadow men and fired a burst on semi-automatic. A bright line of tracer rounds leaped across the darkness from our position to theirs. Tracers.

Tracer rounds are bullets that light up. When the round leaves the chamber, the phosphorus/magnesium/barium salts packed into the gunpowder are ignited to create the glow. They are quite useful for accuracy when firing a machine gun. You watch where the tracers are impacting and adjust fire accordingly. In the case of a semi-automatic rifle like our M16 where we seldom fired it on "burst," a tracer round was loaded into the clip near the bottom. That way you would know when you were about to run out of ammo.

Days before, Ramaglia thought it might be fun to load an entire magazine with tracer rounds just to see what would happen at the next night-fire exercise. Well, the next night-fire exercise happened to be for real, and those tracer rounds lit up a perfect little illuminated path straight back to the barrel of his M16. Tracers work both ways. The enemy knew exactly where we were now.

Good news was the Somalis didn't have night optics either, so they couldn't aim very well and fired high. It was almost comical as the leaves from the tree we were under fluttered down harmlessly around us. Bad news was the Somalis had grenades. And as everybody knows, you only have to be close with horseshoes and hand grenades.

"Grenade! Grenade! Grenade!" Randy yelled out as the old school, pineapple-looking mini-bomb landed about fifteen feet away.

The three of us instinctively flattened out and became one with the terrain. It exploded in a momentary flash pumping the ground like a big fist sending metal and earth up into the air. The three of us laid there for a second as the dirt fell down. Only this time it wasn't nearly as comical as the fluttering leaves.

I looked over at Randy who was cheek to the sand looking back at me. The smile was gone and was replaced by a very stern look of concern. God made His point. I had a great idea. "What do you say we go inside?" Ramaglia nodded in agreement.

I gave Dejesus the word he was waiting to hear. "Roach, we're moving . . . inside."

"Roger that, Sergeant!"

As the Lil Bird banked around and buzzed the street, we used the diversion to get up and sprint for the door.

"If the enemy is in range, so are you."
(The Infantry Journal)

A couple years ago, I was singing some songs at a fund-raiser for the Special Operations Warrior Foundation. I met a man there named Tony Rinderer. Someone had told me, "Hey, I think that guy over there was one of the pilots in Mogadishu." I thought he looked familiar. So we got to talking. I told Tony how the pilots were our heroes and how I felt bad that we never really got a chance to thank them. After we all got home from Somalia, we all went our separate ways. I told him the same story I just told you, about how Ramaglia, Dejesus, and I were in a whole heap of trouble and we never would have made it off that street if not for those two Little Bird pilots.

As I told the story, I saw Tony's eyes slightly start to water up.

"That was me," he said. "I was the second gunship."

So fifteen years later I properly thanked the man who literally saved my life. I shook his hand, gave him a hug, and bought him a drink. Tony and I are good friends now. But on that night, tearing down the streets of Mogadishu, piloting his AH-6 attack helicopter in blackout mode with NODs on and lights off, Tony did not know me from Adam. He only saw three men with the telltale infrared "glint tape" on the top of our helmets that identified us as friendlies. He saw the masses of Somalis hiding just behind the buildings.

"You guys had no idea how many people you were up against," he would later tell me.

He knew that if he did not do something and do it quickly, those three guys down there were in serious trouble. Chief Warrant Officer Tony Rinderer understood without a doubt that he was the one piece of the puzzle that made everything work. He had a job to do and there were people counting on him. At this moment in time, three lives were absolutely counting on him. If he couldn't save us, then who would? So with complete disregard for his own safety, out of ammunition, and entirely vulnerable to ground fire, Tony put his aircraft in between the advancing enemy and us so that we could use that moment to run to safety. You would think I owed him more than a beer! But between warriors, a sincere thank you will suffice.

**"They call it a million dollar wound.
But the government must keep that money
because I still haven't seen a dime." (Forrest Gump)**

Mike Goodale was shot directly in the buttocks. Of course that made for all kinds of silly jokes which Mike fielded with good humor and was in amazingly good spirits. Goodale was a "forward observer." As an FO, his main responsibility was to talk to the aircraft and call in fire support missions should we need it. Well, we needed it and he wasn't about to let us down, wounded or not. Goodale was on his side talking to the air assets and staying in the fight. His positivity and intestinal fortitude was indicative of the men in that room.

Someone made a smart-aleck comment reminding us that the 3rd of October was the birthday of the 3rd Ranger Battalion. Happy Freakin' Birthday. Some party this turned out to be.

For a while I sat in the silence listening to all that was going on around me. The dark house smelled of ammunition, blood, and the unhealthy stink of sweating bodies pumped full of way too much adrenaline. Guys were whispering. Radios were kept on low volume. All of us were waiting. Waiting for anything. An order to move. A rocket to explode. A helicopter to land. A convoy to arrive.

The wait was, in principle, due to the fact we were bound by the Ranger Creed never to leave a fallen comrade. Chief Cliff Wolcott was one of the pilots of Super 61. He was killed on impact when the armored cockpit collapsed around him. The Air Force PJs at the crash did not have the type of equipment necessary to cut through the Kevlar plates to get his body out. We would have to wait for the rest of the Rangers on the Humvees to regroup and come back for us with the necessary gear.

I say we waited *in principle* because even if we had been able to retrieve Chief Wolcott right away, I'm not certain we could have successfully fought our way back carrying all of our wounded. Most accounts of the battle will tell you at that point we were "trapped" or "pinned down." You will be hard pressed finding anyone of us who will admit to being "pinned down." But given the choice of saying "We're stuck here because we can't make it out on our own," or "We're staying here to fight for a fallen comrade," I would choose the latter. You may think it unnecessary that we would risk the lives of so many to retrieve the body of one man who was already dead. I can understand this logic especially since Cliff's soul was long gone from the suitcase that once housed him.

But the Ranger Creed says, "I will never leave a fallen comrade to fall into the hands of the enemy." I took that oath. I made that vow. A solemn promise between men of honor is the cement that forms the unbreakable bond of brothers in arms. There can be no exceptions lest you destroy the absolute faith in one another this chosen calling demands. Stuck or not stuck, pinned down or not pinned down. It didn't matter. We weren't leaving without Cliff Wolcott's body.

"Momma momma, don't you cry.
Your little boy ain't gonna die."
(from an Army cadence sung at marching pace)

"Long way from singing cadences in Ranger School, huh?" It was Sergeant First Class Norm Hooten, a Delta team leader. He and I went through Ranger School together "back when it was hard." I didn't think he remembered me until he sat down beside me in the darkness. He gave me some words of encouragement and thanked me for helping with Fillmore earlier in the day. Hooten was there when his teammate was killed. He knew I tried to find a medevac, and together he and I helped destroy the building where the shot that killed Earl came from.

It was thoughtful of Sergeant Hooten to sit down and offer some support to a young NCO like myself who might be feeling a bit in over his head. I still felt like a failure for not saving Fillmore, so I appreciated his words.

You always try and emulate the good leaders, so I followed Hooten's example and sat down next to Suranski to offer him some encouraging words of my own. I told him he did a good job out there. I'm not sure I could have made a shot like he made through the window with his M203. Mostly though we sat in silence listening to the radio traffic coming through, trying to make sense of the big picture.

Encouraging others is something we are called to do as believers. Paul asks us to "encourage one another and build each other up" (1 Thess. 5:11). He also instructs us to "carry each others burdens, and in this way you will fulfill the law of Christ" (Gal. 6:2).

As a man I like to believe I can fix anything. But you can't always fix someone else's problems or remedy a particular situation. What you can do is sit with that someone and let them know you support them, that you believe in them, and you are there for them 100 percent and then some. Leadership is inevitably accompanied by difficult situations for those who lead and those who will follow. Use those situations as an opportunity to strengthen your character and instill confidence in those around you.

"Besides pride, loyalty, discipline, heart, and mind, confidence is the key to all the locks."
(Coach Joe Paterno)

For a while things stayed quiet, which didn't mean the Somalis moved away. It only meant they weren't shooting. If you went outside, it was a different story. The house we were in was just one casualty collection point. Spread out down the street there were at least three other CCPs, including the crash site itself where Rangers and Air Force paramedics were fully engaged keeping the wounded alive, keeping each other alive, and keeping the enemy at bay.

Captain Steele was having a difficult time figuring out where the rest of the force was located. By then all the Ranger and Delta teams were scattered down two and half city blocks in four different locations. He wanted to consolidate everyone for better command and control. So it was decided someone would have to go outside and move north up the street to link up with the others. Problem was, leaving the CCP was a little less than fun. A couple Delta operators tried earlier only to have the streets erupt in fire. They came diving back inside. The enemy had us surrounded and were just waiting for us to come out.

In Mark Bowden's book, *Black Hawk Down*, he had a chance to interview some of the Somali fighters who were there that night. They claimed the only reason they didn't use mortars to blow us all to kingdom come was because they thought we were holding a family hostage in one of the buildings and were concerned for their safety. I think that's a bunch of crap.

I saw how very little they valued their women and children, sending them out into the street as spotters, shooters, and human shields. There were instances where gunmen would fire at us and actually hide behind the women. Even if the Somalis cared about the family in our CCP, they never would have gotten off a second mortar round because the Night Stalkers would have been on top of them like white on rice.

When fired, a mortar tube makes a distinctive flash readily seen from the air, especially by pilots who did have night vision devices. The MH-6 gunships reloaded six times each that night and in total fired over 70,000 rounds of mini-gun ammunition and more than one hundred rockets. I am convinced the only reason we were never completely overrun was because of those pilots who flew tirelessly all night long to keep us safe. All eight gunship pilots were awarded the Silver Star. Men like CW05 Randy Jones and CW02 Tony Rinderer, the Little Bird pilots who saved Dejesus, Ramaglia, and me, are surely my heroes.

Sergeant Watson thought going outside was a bad idea and was busy telling Captain Steele just that. But the CO was a stubborn man. Someone would have to go outside and make the link up with the nearest element. Since I had been up and down the line all day, I had a pretty good grip on where the others were so I told Watson my squad would go. His other squad leader, Sergeant Hulst, was wounded. So we got the job by default.

"Suranski?"

"Roger, Sergeant?"

"Get it on. We're going outside."

"What's that, S'rgnt?"

"You heard me. Get it on. We're going outside."

I'm sure he wasn't happy about it. But Suranski knew there was a job to be done. And someone had to do it.

"Roger that, S'rgnt." With that he picked up his weapon and moved toward the door.

Who gets shot first? This is what was going through my head and for me was my first real leadership challenge. We all saw the Delta operators get lit up when they tried to exit the building only to come scrambling back in. The same thing was going to happen to us, so I tried to think the order of movement through in my head. *OK, perhaps the first guy out might catch the bad guys off guard. Maybe, he'll make it down to the next building without getting shot. But the second man is definitely going to get hit. Probably the third man too. Hopefully, the fourth guy will react accordingly and not go out at all.*

I turned to my men. "All right, here's how it's gonna be. Floyd, you're going first. Floyd, look at me. There is a building about thirty yards to the right. Don't stop till you get there, hooah? I'll go second. Suranski, you're with me. Roach, you bring up the rear." I pulled Dejesus aside and told him if I got hit, he was to hold on to Suranski and not let him out into the line of fire.

"Roger, S'rgnt. I got you covered," promised Dejesus.

As we lined up at the door and got ready to move, all I could think about was that scene at the end of *Butch Cassidy and the Sundance Kid*. The two outlaws are surrounded by the Mexicalis. In a last ditch effort of bravado and desperation, they come busting out of their hideout with guns blazin'. The movie ends on a freeze frame, but I'm guessing it didn't work out so well for ole Butch and the kid named Sundance.

"OK, here we go. One ... two ... three!"

I heard a lot of gunshots, but I don't know if it was Rangers covering for us or gunmen shooting at us. Probably a lot of both. Somehow we all got out the door without being riddled by bullets and, at a mad dash, made it up to the next intersection.

The rule of thumb when moving under fire is, "I'm up. He sees me. I'm down." That is the maximum time you want to stay exposed to the enemy when running for cover. But there was nothing to hide behind except a dead donkey lying in the street. You take cover where you can find it, when you can find it. So I told Floyd to "get down behind the donkey!" I have to admit, I laughed because Ranger Floyd looked kind of silly with his SAW machine gun propped up on the ass end of a dead ass.

I looked around to get accountability of my guys. Dejesus and Suranski ducked into the narrow alley between the building I was now in front of and the CCP house we just ran from. And there, much to my surprise, kneeling behind a tree not nearly wide enough to offer any real protection was Sergeant First Class Watson. If he was here with us, who was in charge of the platoon?

Young Sergeant Ramaglia, who had voluntarily taken over for his squad when his squad leader Sergeant Hulst was injured, had basically just been promoted to platoon sergeant. Randy told me right before my men and I moved out of the CCP, Sergeant Watson turned to him and said, "Ramaglia, you've got the house. The house is yours."

Watson didn't ask the captain to look after us. He didn't go to the Delta team leader and ask him, "Hey Hooten, would you mind keeping an eye on my guys for me? I have to go outside and I might not come back." He didn't even ask the most senior Ranger in the platoon. He asked the best man for the job.

That's a heck of a responsibility to throw at someone. It's also a heck of a compliment. If anyone could handle the task at hand, it was Randy Ramaglia of 1st Platoon, Bravo Company of the 3rd Ranger Battalion. Sergeant First Class Watson, the Panama combat veteran and man in charge, turned his platoon over to an E-5, first-time NCO, and then followed another one out the door into the hailstorm.

Sergeant First Class Watson really had no business being out there with us. He was too valuable as a platoon sergeant and was needed in the CCP more than in the street trying to complete a linkup. But as the man giving the orders, I don't think he felt right about sending his men out into the kill zone, especially if something were to happen to any one of them. That's an order he did not want to make and would not have wanted to live with. A good leader will never ask you to do what he is not willing to do himself. I hold Sean Watson in the highest respect for making the choice to follow us into the street.

You know what I remember most about the man at that moment as he tried to make himself as skinny as the tree? He wasn't barking orders. He wasn't pointing which way to go. He had become a rifle-man in my squad, waiting for my direction to move. The lesson in humility I learned from Sergeant Watson was powerful. A good leader is also a great follower. To lead is to serve. Remember that. Every single outstanding leader that ever was, is, and shall be under-stands that greatness is found in serving.

As the president and CEO of the United Service Organization, my friend Sloan Gibson has made enormous contributions to the well-being of our military personnel and their families. I've seen the USO centers at our biggest bases and our tiniest forward operat-ing bases throughout the Middle East. They are incredible facilities and they are state of the art. You can watch the latest movie. Unwind with every video game imaginable. You can even read a book to your kid and videotape it so your child back home gets a chance to see her mom or dad before she goes to bed at night. Most importantly, those centers give you a way to stay connected to home. The USO provides free phone calls and internet to all our men and women stationed overseas. When AT&T charged the USO too much to offer this free service to our military, Sloan found a way to raise money to buy their own phone network. He's overseen the creation and construction of two multi-million-dollar family centers here in the States. If you have a loved one who is wounded in combat, it almost always requires a lengthy rehabilitation stay at one of our military hospitals. The new USO centers were created for family members who need some place to call their own while they wait out the long rehab process of their wounded warrior.

If you ask Sloan about what keeps him motivated to do so much more than is asked of him, he will tell you the answer is simple, "The USO is a charitable service organization. So we continually ask our-selves, who needs us the most? Clearly our deployed troops in harm's way and their families are at the top of our list. Who needs us the most and how can we serve them best? That's what drives every decision I make and every program we put in place."

I'd like to think Sloan's extraordinary success on behalf of the USO is due to his Ranger tab he earned as a young infantry officer "back when it was hard" in '75. But as the humble leader I know him to be, Sloan will most likely credit all the people to his left and to his right who set the example for others to follow.

If you don't have an example like Sloan Gibson in your life, I can give you another great leader who lived the concept of servitude as a leadership principle—Jesus Christ. The prophet Zechariah told the people to "shout in triumph" because the greatest leader they'd ever known was en route. "He is righteous and victorious, yet he is humble . . . riding on a donkey's colt" (Zech. 9:9 NLT). A humble man does not have to be a pushover. Jesus was a warrior, a leader of men, a king of kings. If anyone had the right to pull rank and claim entitlement, it would have been the Son of God. And yet, "he is humble." At the last supper why do you think He washed everyone's feet? In this way He could show by His actions what He had told His disciples earlier,

> "Whoever desires to become great among you, let him be your servant. And whoever desires to be first among you, let him be your slave—just as the Son of Man did not come to be served, but to serve." (Matt. 20:26–28 NKJV)

The man talked the talk. The man walked the walk.

So there we were, the five of us, out in the street where no one wanted to be, with nothing more than a dead donkey and a tree for cover. We needed to move. I was just about to get up and make another sprint across the intersection to the next building, when I heard a voice from above.

"Hey Rangers! What are you doing? Get inside." It was a Delta operator leaning out of the window behind me. Turns out, the donkey house we ran to was occupied by another Delta team. God definitely did not want me in the street.

"Let's go. We're moving inside." I didn't have to tell anyone twice. Floyd left his furry friend behind and we all climbed in through a hole that was blown out of a sidewall. We were now in an open-aired courtyard with Sergeant First Class Paul Howe's Delta team. It was the same building Earl Fillmore was pulled into when he was shot. His body was still there and was eerily laid out straight so it could still be carried once rigamortis set in. This is where we would stay the night waiting for the convoy to arrive. This is where I would find out my best friend Casey Joyce was dead. This is where I thought I would die.

"Greater love has no one than this, that one lay down his life for his friends." (John 15:13 NASB)

If you ask anyone what they were thinking during the quiet moments of that night, most will tell you sooner or later they had came to peace with the fact that, "If I die here, I die here. But I'll be damned if it's gonna happen to the man next to me." Men will fight for a cause. But they will die for each other.

By now the long night was beginning to feel like the everlasting night. It had been almost five hours since the sun went down and the enemy came out. And still no word about when the Reaction Force would come back for us or if we would try and fight our way back on our own. I was out of water, out of adrenaline, and out of sorts trying to make sense of how it came down to this. Here I was huddled up with America's finest, in a dirty courtyard of a dirty house in a dirty third-world country sitting next to the lifeless body of a slain super-hero. *Man,* I thought to myself, *if my friends could see me now.* The foggy dream that was home seemed a galaxy away.

Sergeant Watson and I were talking in hushed voices and he wanted to see my ammo clip—the one with the bullet hole in it from when I was hit by the ricocheting wall-following rounds. That took place so long ago I almost forgot it happened. As I handed him the piece of metal that probably saved my life, I thought, *Man, have I been lucky today!* He took a look at it and said, "Yep, Sergeant Thomas, that'll make a good souvenir one day . . . if you survive this one."

If I survive? Wow. Thanks for the vote of confidence, I thought. But as usual, Sean Watson was right. If I survive. Would I? Who knows? That was in God's hands now.

Once you have made peace with God, whatever fear you had of dying is gone. I know because, in the calm of the storm, my mind thought of other things. The things I loved. I thought of Liesa and playing Scrabble in her living room. *Yes, Liesa, RPG is a word.* I thought of singing "Bring Me a Higher Love" with Sonlight Choir back at Trinity United Methodist Church in my hometown of Gainesville, Florida. I thought about a funny story my dad once told me about his radio operator hiding under a table during a mortar attack in Vietnam. I thought about a Valentine's card my mom made for my sister and me. I thought about my buddy Casey and all his plans we talked about the night before.

We were given a chance to make one phone call back to the States. I tried to telephone Liesa but couldn't get her, so I gave my allotted time to Casey. He was waiting to call his wife Deanna. "Well, how's D?" I asked. "What did she have to say?"

"She says she loves me," Casey replied with a smile.

He told me when he finished his enlistment, he was going to get out and move Deanna back to Texas where she would be happy. He never got the chance.

Casey was shot earlier in the day when he was helping to evacuate Private Blackburn, the Ranger who fell from the rope. During the night, while listening to the radio traffic, I pieced together our situation and the extent of our casualties. I heard that weapon's platoon had a KIA. No one told me specifically it was Casey Joyce. I just knew. The heart always knows the truth.

"It is only with the heart that one can see rightly;
What is essential is invisible to the eye."
(The Little Prince)

I suppose everyone was lost in their own thoughts of home because it got quiet for a while. But like an unwelcomed alarm clock blowing an air horn in your ear, I was jolted out of my day dreams, night dreams, or whatever you would call them, and rocked back into reality by an RPG hitting the building. I guess the enemy woke up too.

The Little Bird overhead immediately made a gun pass to eliminate the threat, but he was shooting at the wrong building. Dejesus was standing on a 50-gallon drum staring over the wall when the rocket hit. He saw exactly where it came from. So one of the Delta men got on the radio with the pilot and told them to "Follow de Roach!" Dejesus used the tracer rounds of his SAW machine gun to precisely mark the enemy's position. Following his lead, the Little Bird came in right over our heads with rockets and this time made quick disposal of the enemy position. Way to go, Roach!

The Bronze Star he received for his efforts that day would read, "Specialist Dejesus' actions reflect great credit upon himself, the 3rd Ranger Battalion, and the entire United States Army." I'm glad he was on our side.

After a while, sometime around midnight, the radio at last relayed the information we had all been waiting to hear. "The Quick Reaction Force is leaving the compound," we were told.

Finally! I thought. *Maybe they'll get here in time to get Jamie Smith out of here before he bleeds to death.* Corporal Smith was shot in the groin severing his femoral artery. The wound was too high for a tourniquet, so the men in that CCP took turns all night with their hands down inside his leg, trying desperately to stop the bleeding. The Delta Special Forces medic was miraculously keeping Jamie alive on IV fluids and sheer willpower.

Somewhere way off on the other side of Mogadishu, we could hear the distant sounds of gunfire as the long multinational force began to make its way toward us.

It won't be long now, I thought. *Thank God. This thing is almost over.*

"We are pressed on every side by troubles, but we are not crushed. We are perplexed, but not driven to despair. We are hunted down, yet never abandoned by God. We get knocked down, but we are not destroyed."
(2 Corinthians 4:8–9 NLT)

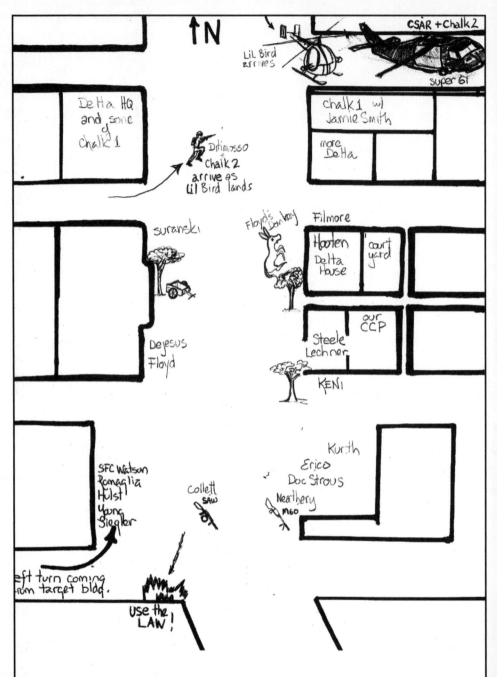

Hand-drawn battle scene by author/soldier Keni Thomas. Complete with placement of key buildings, hostile forces, and a donkey that was in the wrong place at the wrong time.

Chapter 9

THE MILE

*I accept the fact that as a Ranger, my country expects me to move
further, faster, and fight harder than any other soldier.*

—2ND STANZA OF THE RANGER CREED

"YOU GOT ANY WATER?" I asked the medic from the 10th Mountain
Division.

It was only supposed to be an hour-long mission so I thought
I'd save the weight and left the canteens back on my bunk along
with my night vision. By the time the relief convoy got to us around
0230, it was almost twelve hours later. I was dehydrated, exhausted,
and downright smoked. With the arrival of the 10th Mountain
and the rest of the Quick Reaction Force, I finally began to relax and
could feel my energy draining away. The adrenaline that kept my
body going all night started turning into lactic acid and was sinking

heavily into my muscles like sludge settles to the bottom of an engine when you shut it down.

The Quick Reaction Force was everything and anything but quick. There were soldiers from the 10th Mountain Division, which was the regular-Army infantry unit doing duty in Mogadishu as part of the U.N. security force. There were Malaysian armored personnel carriers, Pakistani tanks, Apache helicopters, Navy SEALs, and of course, what was left of our Ranger buddies on the Humvees including Ranger cooks, mechanics, medics, bakers, and candlestick makers. It became an international force of considerable size presenting a substantial organizational challenge for the people trying to wrangle it together. "Quick" was simply not part of the equation.

It's a good thing Task Force Ranger had all the help, though. Most of our vehicles were toast. They were chewed up, mutilated, and spit out by ambush after ambush the day before. The original Ranger Ground Reaction Force that pulled up to the target building and loaded the prisoners was now down to half its original strength. The last I saw of those guys was when they drove away from the target building almost twelve hours before. Once they left the objective and headed back to the airfield, their convoy was besieged by the entire city of Mogadishu and the rest of hell came along to add to the carnage.

When Super 61 went down, the ground force tried to navigate their way back to us through the maze of alleys and side streets. But the constant barrage of small arms fire and rocket propelled grenades became overwhelming. Shot up and blown apart, most of the vehicles were running on rims, prayers, and a whole lot of *"come on baby . . . you can make it."* One was even dragging an axle and was pushed back to base by a five-ton truck. Big, heavy, slow-moving vehicles running on no tires become easy targets.

Men were going down fast. Private First Class Richard Kowaleski was killed in the driver's seat when a rocket came right through the door of the five-ton truck he was driving. My roommate Dominick Pilla was dead. My friend from my very first squad in the Ranger Regiment, Sergeant Lorenzo Ruiz, was also shot while manning the gun turret of his Humvee. He died on the operating table. One of my best friends, John Burns, was hit in the leg twice by rounds from an AK-47. It shattered the lower part of his tibia; he would spend a good portion of the next two years in physical rehab recovering. Master Sergeant Tim "Griz" Martin, a Delta veteran, was also a demolitions and explosives expert. In an ironic twist of fate, he would die in the explosion when an RPG blew up his vehicle. His wounds were irrecoverable.

Like a jackhammer on concrete, piece by piece, man by man, ambush after ambush gradually took its toll until the convoy began to fall apart. Wounded Rangers were in the back of trucks piled on top of dead ones, who were thrown on top of Somali POWs, who were lying on top of dead Somalis caught in the cross fire. Eventually the ground force became so ineffective, they had no choice but to abandon their effort to save us and turned instead to saving themselves. They headed back to base.

Vehicles can be replaced. Lives cannot.

Like a gruesome scene from an over-the-top episode of *ER*, the field hospital back at the air base was in full combat trauma mode as more than thirty shot-up and blown-up fighters were brought in all at once. Doctors and nurses scrambled to prioritize the wounded and stabilize the critically injured. That staff performed magnificently under the most stressful circumstances. Their actions that day undoubtedly saved lives. Medics—they are truly the angels of war.

The men who survived that hell and were still capable of fighting were given no time to decompress, to talk about it, to grieve, or even to make sense of what just happened to them. All they had time to do was to off-load the wounded, wash the blood and guts out of the back of their vehicles, and reload. They were going back in. Having made it out of that nightmare, these men were being asked once again to "get it on" and willingly return to the killing fields as part of a hastily assembled rescue force.

Staff Sergeant Jeff Struecker, by default, was now the NCO in charge. It became his responsibility to get his men refitted, reloaded, and reorganized. As a combat veteran of Panama, Struecker knew exactly what everyone was feeling, because he was feeling it too. They were scared. It was Ranger Brad Thomas who stepped up and voiced what all brave men must come to grips with admitting, "If I go in there, I might not make it back."

As the man who always set an example for others to follow, Struecker who would one day fittingly become a chaplain, then gave the sermon of his life. He told those young men that it's OK to be afraid. "Lord knows I'm afraid too," Jeff confessed. "But there is a big difference between being scared and being a coward. This," he added, "is what we all signed up to do. There are people out there counting on you. Now what are you going to do about it?"

The best sermons are lived, not preached. Staff Sergeant Struecker reloaded, suited up, and climbed back into his Humvee. Nobody would have blamed any of those men had they opted out. But not a single one stayed back. They all volunteered, they all suited up. Despite their extreme mental and physical fatigue, found their character, stepped forward, and answered again. One man, Ranger Dale Sizemore, even cut a cast off of his arm so he wouldn't be told he was medically unable to fight.

Why would men risk their lives fully knowing the hazards of what was waiting for them? Because they had brothers out there counting on them, that's why. *Never shall I fail my comrades.* It was a promise and an oath we all made to each other and was never to be taken lightly.

"Some say a hero was born to be brave.
But I'm here to tell you a hero
is a scared man who won't walk away."
(from the song "Hero" by Keni Thomas)

That initial Ranger rescue team left the airfield at about 1700, while it was still daylight. Staff Sergeant Struecker had the lead vehicle. They made it all of a hundred yards out of the gate when they were hammered by intense small arms fire from the left side and were forced to turn back. My good friend, Sergeant Raleigh Cash, was part of that element and had command of his own Humvee fitted with a .50-caliber machine gun.

As the overwhelmed rescue team tried to turn around and pull back to the compound, Cash was frantically shooting out the passenger window engaging targets. "ACTION LEFT! ACTION LEFT!" he called out repeatedly. Somalis on rooftops were shooting. People in doorways and windows were shooting. Specialist Lepre was up in the gun turret methodically pounding back with the big .50-cal.

The noise was insane. Muzzle flashes were blinking everywhere like some nightmarish red carpet attack of the paparazzi. Rounds were impacting the sides of the Humvee. Thanks to Lepre who was totally exposed, they pushed through the ambush only to get hit immediately at the next turn. And then Sergeant Cash did something peculiar. He put his weapon down, leaned back in the seat, and stopped firing. Raleigh called it his "Ahh Haa" moment.

Raleigh told me, "When we hit the second ambush, I just stopped shooting and turned the world off for a second. I was thinking, *I'm gonna die here. We're probably all going to die here. I don't think any of us are going to make it.* I thought about that for a second and figured, *Well, if I got shot in the arm or the leg, it would hurt like hell, but the Doc would fix me up and I'd be OK. If I got shot in the head, I wouldn't know it anyway.*"

So Raleigh Cash accepted his fate and did what most of us would do when death comes calling and is staring us in the face.

"I made my peace with God," he said. "I was an Airborne Ranger. This is what I was meant to do. This is where I was supposed to be. If God wanted me to die in a fight, then so be it. Once I accepted that, I became calm, and honestly I wasn't afraid any more."

Sergeant Cash was back in the fight. He picked up his Car-15 rifle, leaned out the window, and began engaging the swarming Somalis. (Remember all this is happening within a hundred yards outside the gates of the "safe zone.")

"We kept having to zigzag through the cross streets to try and get back because they were throwing up quick ambushes at every turn," Raleigh explained. "So about the fourth time we got lit up, the side of my truck got peppered. That's when I felt it hit me."

Something came through the door and jabbed him in the leg. "I thought I'd been shot," Raleigh said. He reached down fully expecting to feel blood but there was none. Cash would later find the tip of a bullet poking through the passenger side door. The bullet resistant glass did its job.

In one of the military's after-action reports that mentions Sergeant Cash and his actions that day, it credited the bullet resistant glass and Kevlar equipment with saving him from "serious if not lethal injury." Raleigh will tell you the credit lies elsewhere.

"When I looked down and saw the hole in the side of the door where the round was lodged, I was thanking God, not the door."

Fortunately for my friend Raleigh, on that very morning on the third of October, before anything went down, and for no particular reason, he decided it might be a good idea to put the armored doors on the vehicles. If you think God isn't watching out for you, you are mistaken.

As hard and courageous as Rangers like Cash, Sizemore, and Brad Thomas were, there was just no way they could make it across the city on their own. They needed help. The 10th Mountain Division was alerted. Help was on the way.

"Have I not command you? Be strong and courageous! . . . for the LORD your God is with you wherever you go." (Joshua 1:9 NASB)

The 10th Mountain brought an entire company of fresh infantry soldiers and some Apache attack helicopters. Unfortunately they didn't bring any armored vehicles like Bradleys or M1 Abrahams tanks, which would have laughed at small arms fire and RPGs. But the Bradleys, Abrahams, and the ever so lethally-accurate Spectre gunships were all back home in the garage because Les Aspin, the appointed defense secretary, denied the U.S. Army its original request for armor and Spectre air support.

Perhaps Aspin's decision would have been different had Sergeant First Class Watson been invited to that meeting. Our platoon sergeant could have reminded the defense secretary that "It's better to have and not need, than to need and not have." We needed and did not have. So America's mighty and well-funded military had to go ask for help from Malaysia and Pakistan, who arrived with their Armored

Personnel Carriers, which they called BTRs, and two very old T-48 Tanks respectively.

It took almost five hours to wrangle up the multinational relief convoy of more than three hundred men and a dozen vehicles. Once it was put together, the people in charge, like Major Nixon of the command center, then had to come up with a plan and an order of movement. Coordinating it all took time. Time is a precious commodity when the life is bleeding out of one of your comrades, Jamie Smith, and he's out there somewhere in the dark holding on to the hope that help is on the way.

Meanwhile, stinking of exhaustion, sweat, and blood, holed up in the dark of some frightened Somali family's home in the middle of a dirty, third-world city on the eastern coast of a disparate African nation, we waited for news of the QRF's arrival. The radio kept playing mind tricks with us all night. It was like being on the receiving end of a cruel joke.

2030: "The QRF is leaving the compound in approximately one hour." *(Thank God.)*

2130: "The QRF is delayed. Should be leaving the compound in about an hour." *(Figures.)*

2240: "QRF is leaving the compound." *(Thank God.)*

2300: "QRF is back at the compound." *(What?)*

2330: "QRF is leaving the compound." *(Yeah, whatever.)*

"The train is leaving the station."

"The chair is behind the door."

"The ice cream man has snacks for you all."

It was getting ridiculous and I was getting delirious. The Quick Reaction Force needed a new name. *What's taking so long? This is slower than a turtle stampede.* But once again, we didn't know how bad they had it. On their first attempt through the city, the convoy came under attack and got jammed up at the K4 traffic circle in the center of Mogadishu. They were turned back and had to reroute. This time it was easy to track their progress. Forget the radio updates. All you had to do was listen to the volume of gunfire coming from across the city. The louder it got, the closer they were. At around 0200 in the morning on Monday 4 October, the first elements of the rescue convoy finally reached the crash site.

They turned the corner toward us about a block to my right on Mahdale Road, the same cross street as the courtyard we were in. Because these were soldiers and foreign fighters that had not trained with us, we were extra cautious with the linkup so we didn't shoot each other. I thought it would be a shame if I made it through the long night only to be shot in the morning by some nervous private from a friendly unit.

By the time the last of the convoy rounded the corner, the eastern sky behind them was beginning to show signs of a new day. The black of night was giving way to the purples and oranges of the early morning. The third of October was behind us.

I thought about what Sergeant Watson said to me earlier. *Maybe I might "survive this" after all.*

"Don't be afraid, for I am with you. Don't be discouraged, for I am your God. I will strengthen you and help you. I will hold you up with my victorious right hand." (Isaiah 41:10 NLT)

"Wake up! Wake up! The Americans are still here!"

There they were again, the voices chanting their foreign gibberish. As the sun came up, the Muslim morning call to prayer could be heard echoing in the distance from mosques throughout the city. To us, the words we did not understand could only be imagined as sounding more like a battle cry than a prayer:

"Arise, all you children of Islam, your god needs you! Especially the ones with RPGs! It's Monday. A good day to go kill the infidels before they get away. Wake up! Wake up!"

Just because the day was new didn't mean the Somalis had gone home. The bad guys were still there. The threat was still very real. Sergeant First Class Watson was understandably concerned about the armored personnel carriers parked right outside the CCP. We started packing them full of our wounded, but it was taking a long time.

"Hey! How about we get those RPG magnets out of the way?" Watson strongly suggested.

It was more an order than a request. Sometimes though, despite your best intentions, "yelling more loudlier" will not always move things "more quicklier." It took time to load the incapacitated men, like Lieutenant Lechner, onto stretchers and carry them out to the vehicles. It took time to help a guy like Pete Neathery, who had multiple IVs sticking out of his good arm, to climb through the armored door opening. It took time to get all those wounded men evacuated, and on top of that, we were running out of space.

The 10th Mountain soldiers had our backs. Literally. They pulled security enabling us to focus on getting our wounded comrades moved into the BTRs. I remember feeling particularly good about one of their men, a big black guy with a booming voice, probably a platoon sergeant or a first sergeant. He had some experience under his belt. You could tell, because he was squaring his men away left and right.

"Stay alert! Watch your sectors! Get down over there! Use your heads!"

Time was ticking. And ticking sounds like a timer rigged to a bomb, which means something is going to explode soon. And sure enough, an RPG came smoking across the street and impacted another building. There's nothing like an exploding rocket to wake you up in the morning. Whatever tiredness and exhaustion we were feeling would have to be ignored. Time to get it on. Again.

By about 0500 hours most of the casualties were loaded and the Malaysian BTRs were ready to go. But we couldn't leave yet. The guys at the crash were still working to free Chief Wolcott's body from the wreckage. They tried to pull the cockpit apart with two Humvees. If they could loosen its grip just a bit, it might be enough to slide the body out. But cutting the aircraft around the body wasn't working and time had run out. Finally, a decision had to be made no one wanted to make.

During the San Francisco earthquake, an elevated highway collapsed crushing cars and all the people beneath it. There was a small child who was still alive but pinned under the body of her mother who did not survive. EMT rescuers had to cut the mom in half in order to save the child. After the earthquake in Haiti, there was so much rubble and concrete several field amputations were required just to extract the living and the dead. The burden of leadership requires some very difficult decisions to be made. It isn't fair. It isn't right. But there it is and what are you going to do about it?

I hope the man who was tasked with that gruesome job knows he did the absolute right thing and he has peace in knowing Cliff Wolcott's soul was long gone and feeling no pain. That medic did what he had to do and on behalf of all the men of Task Force Ranger, he fulfilled our solemn promise to "never leave a fallen comrade to fall into the hands of the enemy."

The body of Chief Cliff "Elvis" Wolcott was now recovered. It was time to go. The sensitive items aboard the wreck were scuttled so they didn't fall into the wrong hands. Since there was no more room in the APCs, the bodies of the KIA were tied down on top. It didn't seem right, but the priority was obviously to the living. It was a surreal site and a sobering reminder of what we had been through and what still might be waiting for us.

Finally, four hours after the convoy arrived, we were ready to leave that place and head for home. We said our "See ya laters" to our wounded friends and thanked the guys from the 10th Mountain for their help. We began regrouping to move out.

The plan was to transport everyone to a safe zone at an old soccer stadium about a mile away. There the wounded would be triaged and air-lifted back to base where the world's best docs and medics were already frantically at work trying to save the lives of the wounded from the ambushed convoys the day before. These angels of war were about to get hit with another wave.

"Run, Forrest! Run!" (from the movie *Forrest Gump*)

"Doug! What are you doing here?!"

The last I saw of Doug Boren was at the target building the day before. He was running off with the Delta medic, holding a bleeding neck. For some reason, I just assumed they got him out somehow before we lost contact with the Humvees. But here he was. Still alive! He had a dirty bandage on his neck and the vest he wore that held all his 203 grenades was empty, meaning he fought all night just like us.

In fact, the entire time Doug was less than 30 feet away in the building across the street from Floyd's dead donkey.

"Good to have you back, buddy!" I said with a smile.

Since all the vehicles were full of wounded Rangers, the rest of us would move on foot. The idea being we could use the vehicles as cover. Kinda like what you used to see in those old WWII films where Patton's foot soldiers would run along crouching behind the tanks.

Now, I'm a pretty fast guy and was in excellent shape. But I was hard-pressed to keep up with a nervous Malaysian armored-vehicle driver who put the pedal to the metal as soon as incoming rounds started *tink-tink-tinking* off the side of his ride. On top that, all of us were now humping double our normal load, after picking up the weapons of our wounded comrades.

In addition to the fifty pounds of gear strapped to my body, I had my rifle, a shotgun, and Neathery's M-60 machine gun including rounds. I had already exhausted my lifetime supply of adrenaline the night before. The only thing carrying any of us was intestinal fortitude and God. The vehicles drove away and we were left in the dust.

The Mogadishu Mile, as it came to be called, was the first point in the battle where, in hindsight, my emotions began to get the best of me. I was admittedly scared at the seemingly inevitable reality that some of us, including myself, might not make it out of here. We did the right thing. We stayed and fought all night to honor our promise to a fallen comrade and now we're gonna pay for it with our lives? Wouldn't that just be typical? Do the right thing and get nailed for it. So yeah, I was nervous. And I was angry.

I went on a silent rampage to no one in particular. "This is it? This is the best they can freakin' do? We're the Rangers! These are Delta operators. They can't come up with a ride for us? We have to run out of here? I could have done that last night!"

Of course, I didn't know the whole picture. I only knew my little world. I still did not know a second bird was shot down less than a mile away and there was no one left to get to it. I did not know—as I would later learn—that a total of five MH-60s ultimately became inoperable from the small arms damage they incurred while flying all night to support us.

Even the *Gunslinger* was out of action. Not too long after it got dark, one of the CCPs put in an urgent request for a resupply. With all the casualties, the Air Force PJ Tim Wilkinson was running out of IV fluids and medical supplies. Ranger Carlos Rodriguez was critically wounded, and Wilkinson was doing everything he could to keep the young man alive.

To make matters worse, with all the enemy massing in the area, the Rangers at that CCP who could still shoot were running through their ammo faster than Sherman rolled through Georgia. Someone had to get in there and deliver the goods or those men were done. Super 66 got the call. The crew loaded up the supplies and flew right back into the hornet's nest.

Can you imagine what our pilots Chief Wood and Chief Fuller were thinking? They knew exactly what was waiting for them out there. That drop zone was hotter than the devil's armpits and they knew they were gonna take a licking. But people were counting on them and it was literally up to them to deliver. If they didn't, who would? You don't have to like it. You don't have to be happy about it. But what are you going to do about it?

By now it was dark and as per SOP, all the Night Stalkers were flying in blackout mode. The pilots and crew wear night-vision goggles that makes them look like spooky cyber warriors with green glowing eyes. CW3 Stan Wood knows he has to take in a resupply but he has no idea where he's going. The last he saw of the battlefield was a few hours earlier when he roped us in at the target building in broad day-light. Super 66 had been in a holding pattern ever since. Stan called in over the radio "Hey, where am I going?" Keith Jones answered with a "Follow me." Remember, he was the Little Bird pilot of Star 41 who had made the daring rescue at the crash site earlier that day. Keith would shine the infrared search light on the building where the resup-plies were needed. Through his NODs Stan would be able to see the IR search light as plain as day.

"Once Keith lit up the roof top and I knew where I was going," Stan recalls, I told the guys, 'OK, here we go.' As I made the approach I could see someone standing in the doorway with an IR strobe. So I was confident we were in the right location."

Stan Wood and Gary Fuller flared in over the street, held that bird in a hover just four feet over the roof and, like a horse in the rain, stood there and took it as small arms fire *clink-clink-clinked* around them. Ned "No Fear" Norton was on the right side and fired off a quick burst with the mini-gun. Staff Sergeant Scott Hargis was the gunner on the left side and seconds later opened up on full cyclic at 6,000 rounds per minute. "It was a beautiful sound," Stan told me.

In the 20 seconds they were on station in a hover, SSG. Hargis fired over 1,700 rounds of 7.62 ammunition. Someone came over the radio and simply stated the truth about that moment, "Good shooting!"

Stan Wood called in, "Resupply Complete."

The men on the ground could fight on. Super 66 dragged itself back to the airfield. Chief Wood told me later when he landed and inspected the damage, all the oil and transmission fluid was gone. He counted over forty bullet holes in the fuselage. How they made it back alive was a miracle. The *Gunslinger* was out of the fight.

Task Force Ranger started the mission with eight Black Hawks. By the next morning there were three left. At ten million and a few hundred thousand dollars apiece to the taxpayers, gambling what was left of the MH-60s was not a bet the command group was willing to make in order to get us a ride. As Gerry Izzo, one of the pilots for Super 65, would later recount, "the time for helicopters had passed." The forty or so of us left in the city would not be flying or even riding back; we would have to foot it. This time though, we weren't running to help someone else. We were running for our lives. And that's exactly what we did. Shooting the entire way.

"You and you, panic. The rest of you come with me."
(attributed to a Marine Corps Gunnery Sergeant)

I started getting nervous when I realized we weren't following any sort of Ranger tactics other than "Run for it!" We would pause at intersections for a scroll to the road, but only as a formality. Not many guys were actually taking time to watch down both ends of the road. Basically they'd take a knee and start firing, even if there wasn't a target. If someone down there was even thinking about stepping out and shooting at us, a barrage of rounds might discourage them. I even saw our CO running and shooting up at windows, then dropping his empty magazine and leaving it on the ground as he kept moving.

First of all, you never purposely leave equipment. *And care of equipment shall set the example for others to follow.* Secondly, just what exactly is it you think you are going to hit while running and gunning? I'll tell you what you are going to hit, two things—diddly and squat. I started picking up the empty magazines, as if it would erase the sins of the sinners and we would all be pardoned and allowed to live.

Not once in our training in Fort Benning or in the sand dunes of Somalia had we ever practiced clearing by fire while crossing an intersection or running and gunning while moving down a street. People were doing stupid things. They were scared. The enemy knew it and was pouring on the fear. If left unchecked, fear will lead to panic. And panic makes you forget your training, forget the plan, and leaves those around you hung out to dry.

I wanted to yell, "STOOOOOOOPP!" thinking it might somehow make everyone come to a halt, take a deep breath, and correct their wrongful ways. But the train kept moving and all I could do was keep up.

"Sergeant Thomas!" Floyd was trying to warn me.

He saw two Somalis step out into an alley with RPGs aimed right at us. At least Floyd was still paying attention. He shouldered his SAW machine gun and let loose with a burst of 5.56 neutralizing the threat before they could to the same to us. David Floyd had surely just saved our lives.

Good shot, Floyd! How wrong had I been? The very same guy I had once tried to get rid of, ended up being the one who saved us all. Man, I am glad we held David to a higher standard. I am glad he did so as well. You may never know the people you reach by the example you set. But rest assured, the actions you choose to take or not to take, affect lives.

Honestly, at this point I didn't know where we were going. Like Forrest Gump I just kept running until someone told us to stop. From our start position at the crash site, we ran all the way back to the original target building following the same route we had used the day before. We then turned left at the intersection I roped in at and ran south down the main road fittingly called Armed Forces Drive. The Olympic Hotel was now on our right. Who would want to stay there? I thought. We kept running for another half dozen blocks then hung a left toward the east. That's when someone finally said, "Stop!"

There were a couple Humvees and one of the old Pakistani T-48 tanks in the middle of the road. We all ducked into an area that looked like a carport and was surrounded by a two-foot wall. We could use it for cover while we caught our breath.

Randy Ramaglia was cussing. Biblically speaking, some will tell you there's a difference between cursing and swearing. Both are a form of prayer really. When you swear, you make an oath. As in "Lord, if You get us out of this, I swear I'll call my mom every Sunday." Cursing would be praying, but in a negative connotation. As in "Lord, please curse this place and these people trying to kill me."

Randy wasn't cursing and he wasn't exactly swearing either. He was cussing, which I think is a little of both. Being a southern boy from the North Carolina mountains, he was pretty good at it, too. He was cussing at the bullet that just tore a hole through the gigantic DAWKIN tattoo on his back. He was cursing the Somali who did it and the mother he came from. He was swearing that after all this, God better not let him get killed running out of this hole. Amen. I second that.

"Dude, you gonna use that?"

Nelson may as well have been asking for the rest of my french fries, he said it so calmly. Sergeant Sean Nelson was Chalk 1's M60 machine gunner. His gun had a bent barrel. The one I was carrying for Neathery did not.

I gladly handed it over. "You can have it. You're way better with it than I am."

Nelson loaded a belt in, laid down behind the wall, propped the gun up in a steady firing position and proceeded to pound the window of a two-story building across the road. He saw someone up there take a shot at us. As soon as Nelson opened fire, that carport area we were in starting ringing like a bad guitar solo feeding back in a library. Man, that gun was loud. It's funny. I don't remember hearing the grenades or the LAW or even the M60 when I got behind it the day before. But I sure remember the sound of Nelson's that morning. No wonder the dude was half deaf.

It also got the attention of the Pakistani tank commander. Either he saw what Nelson was shooting at, or he just wanted to get in the fight. That big ole T-48 gun turret whirred as it made a 180 to face the building. *KAWHAMMM!* The earth shook as he fired off a round. For a second, nothing happened. It looked like the building coughed or hiccupped. And then, like a trap door just opened, the whole thing collapsed.

"Dude!" yelled Nelson. "That tank just took out the whole freakin' building!"

Wow. I was thinking. *That was cool. I've got to get me one of those!* The T-48 may have been as old as the state of Alabama, but it still packed a punch.

I'm sure I was not alone in my thinking. Man, why didn't we have tanks like that? Can you imagine what we could have done with the M1 Abrams we originally requested from Washington? In the words of General Montgomery the U.S. force Commander in Somalia, those M1s would have allowed us to "punch straight through to the Rangers." I don't need a general to tell me that. I know if we would have had tanks at our disposal the night before, or even a Bradley fighting vehicle, we could have gotten Jamie Smith out a lot sooner, before he bled to death. Hindsight is always 20/20, so they say. That's because everything works out perfectly in retrospect. But there was no time for armchair quarterbacking. We were moving again.

We put as many guys as we could on the couple Humvees from the 10th Mountain and they took off. That left about twenty-five of us including the Delta squadron's sergeant major. I figured if anyone could make something happen, he sure would. You know what his plan was? You guessed it. We're running. Really? I could have thought of that. Here we go again.

There are some details about that run out of the city that are still hazy to me. Over the years, after telling the story so many times and focusing only on certain key elements, my mental hard drive has deleted some of the memories of that morning. But there is one that is still as vivid as if it happened yesterday. It's one of those images you just never forget.

He looked to be about sixty. He was tall and thin, 6'3", maybe 160 pounds. His hair was a little gray and his robe was a light blue. He was wearing sandals and was walking down the other side of the street in the opposite direction as us, oblivious to the fight still raging around him. He knew where he was heading, but he was lost in his own world or so caught up in grief that none of it mattered. In his arms, light enough to carry in front like a bundle of sticks, was a young child, limp and lifeless. It was as if the old man had been walking around the city all night looking for his grandchild, had found who he was looking for, and now he was taking him home. Some of the other guys remember the child being a girl. Looked to me like a boy. But maybe it's because I just didn't want to believe a little girl could have been caught up and spit out in the cross fire of a fight that cared nothing about innocence.

And that's when I first thought about it . . . *My God. How many people did we kill?*

> "There is no honorable way to kill, no gentle way to destroy. There is nothing good in war. Except its ending." (Abraham Lincoln)

"Get in there!" yelled Sergeant Boren. Doug was talking to me.

We ran a few blocks more when two Malaysian BTR carriers came from the east to give us a ride. Finally! But these are ten-man vehicles. We had about twenty-five. So we were shoving people in like circus clowns. As the guy in charge I, of course, made sure my men went first. I was outside the vehicle waving them in when Sergeant Boren got to me.

"Go on," I pointed toward the door hatch.

He looked at me like a mom who'd just been back-talked by her son in church.

"Get in there!" he yelled.

Oh yeah, Sergeant Boren was the squad leader after all. I was in charge for eighteen hours. I'm not sure I was ready to give that up. But a good leader is a good follower when he has to be. You don't have to like it, but you have to know how to do it. Lead. Follow. Or get out of the way. I climbed in the hatch and made my way toward the front behind the driver.

We were overloaded. Guys were sitting on top of each other trying not to panic as the BTR rumbled down the road and the Malaysian gunner in the turret fired away with his AK-47. His partner who was crouched below would load the thirty-round ammo clips and pass them up. The gunner would empty his rounds, lean back down from the portal, get another mag, slap it in, pop back up, and fire away. Since we couldn't see a thing from inside that "RPG magnet," we could only imagine the hordes of Somali gunmen this guy must have been shooting at.

I felt completely helpless, like that guy swimming for the dock as Jaws, the great white shark, is coming for him.

"We're almost there." I kept telling myself. "We're almost there."

And then the vehicle stopped. What? I turned around to see the driver just sitting there. He seemed completely calm. But that's when I truly began to lose it.

Are you freakin' kidding me? We came so far, only to be at the mercy of these clowns in a tin can who don't know how to drive and kept stopping. If speed is security, then not moving at all is surely doomsday. Sergeant First Class Watson was being his usual sarcastic self and it wasn't helping.

"Oh yeah," he started in. "This is great. I can just see an RPG come ripping through this thing any second now." That was about as reassuring as his "if you survive" comment the night before.

By this time everyone's single focus was getting that vehicle moving. Helplessness is a terrible feeling. All we could do is yell, but the driver kept ignoring us. He didn't know what we were saying anyway. He wasn't budging. I ordered Roach to tell the driver to "drive," as if being Puerta Rican meant Dejesus could speak Malaysian.

"I speak Spanish, Sergeant, not Malaysian. He's only doing what they're telling him." Dejesus tried to appease me. It didn't work.

I was getting dangerously anxious and could feel the panic bubbling up in my chest like the famous Alka-Seltzer volcano in a middle school science project. *We gotta go. And we gotta go now!* When the Delta sergeant major chimed in "Get this thing moving!" I couldn't take it anymore. I don't care if the truck in front of us was stopped. Make something happen. Obviously those chumps didn't know who they had in the back of their truck.

I pulled out the twelve-inch field knife my dad gave me for Christmas. He had it engraved with the words *Sgt. Kenneth Thomas*

Bco 3rd Ranger Batt. I thought maybe the driver would like to see what a fine looking knife it was, so I stuck it into his face and said, "Get this thing moving. Now!"

The Roach was already reaching to pull me back and Sergeant Watson calmed me down in a hurry by sitting on my legs. I never said another word. A long two or three miles later, looking up through the gun portal, we passed under the gates outside the soccer stadium.

The BTR came to a halt and shut down its engines. Like a passenger in the back of the plane, I was the last man out as I waited for everyone to un-pile and untangle themselves. My legs fell asleep because Watson was sitting on them. I stumbled out the door and fell to the ground. You know who helped me up? It was the driver. He was smiling and offered me a cigarette. He looked to be about eighty years old and had obviously seen a whole lot of combat in his time. I reached for his hand and as he lifted me up, I told him "Thank you." It was more an apology than an act of politeness. He patted me on the back. I was forgiven.

It was 0830 hours on 4 October, almost eighteen hours since we got the initial call to "get it on" and climbed aboard the *Gunslinger* waiting for the code word *Irene.* As I walked toward the stadium, I realized it was all finally over. My three guys made it. Doug was alive and the squad was whole again. My mission was accomplished. The exhaustion took hold and I started to cry. I was thinking about Casey's wife Deanna. What was I supposed to tell her?

"You OK, Cornbread?" It was Randy Ramaglia.

Here he was with a bullet hole in his back and he was worried about me. I felt bad later for not showing more concern for his wound. But at the time I guess it was enough to know he was alive.

There is a scene in the movie *Platoon* depicting a casualty evacuation site. The wounded men on stretchers are in one row waiting for the medevac helicopter. In another row you see something covered with ponchos. As the helicopter lands, one poncho is blown back by the rotor wash to reveal the lifeless body of someone the soldiers once knew. If you added some surrealism to that scene, like a turban-wearing Indian man serving hot tea on a tray and dusty, bloody soldiers sitting in bleachers, that is exactly what I was looking at. We even had old Vietnam-era Hueys landing on the soccer field to carry out the casualties.

In one row, stretchers were laid out on the 30-yard line as medics and doctors busily moved between the wounded like nannies fussing over their favorite children. People of all nationalities came from the U.N. compound to help. Critically wounded men like Carlos Rodriguez and Jim Lechner were being well cared for as they waited their turn to be transported to the main hospital. Mike Goodale, the man with the million-dollar wound, remembers laying out there on a stretcher talking to Sergeant Raleigh Cash who came over to check in on him.

"So I'm lying there basically naked because they cut my pants off me. All I had covering me was a sheet. I'd lost a fair amount of blood and they were pumping a cold IV into me, so I started shivering. I was drinking a cup of hot tea some Indian guy gave me. Cash and I were talking when I stopped and told him 'I'm cold.' You should have seen the look on his face. Raleigh seriously thought I lost it and was going to die right there."

Someone forgot to tell Sergeant Goodale it was hotter than Hades under the late morning African sun and that a cup of hot tea was not the normal choice of beverage for a man who was right in the head. Raleigh must have thought Mike was going into shock or something.

Sergeant Cash did what any friend would do for someone who said "I'm cold" in 90-degree heat. "I ran around until I found him a blanket."

Goodale and the rest of the wounded waited their turn to be air-lifted off the playing field, a few yards away on the 40-yard line, there was another row of stretchers. They were covered with ponchos. There were no doctors or medics fussing over them.

Sergeant Watson went off to get the bad news. When he gathered the platoon around, that's when we learned the extent of our losses. In my own little world, I knew we lost Jamie Smith. He bled to death waiting for help that could not get there in time. I heard on the radio earlier in the night that "a member" of weapons platoon was killed. The final casualty report confirmed what I already knew in my heart. My best friend Casey Joyce was gone. He would not be taking Deanna back to Texas after all. B company lost four others. My roommate Specialist Pilla, my friend Sergeant Lorenzo Ruiz, Spec. James Cavaco, and Private Richard Kowalewski were all killed while fighting from the vehicles.

Floyd knew I was close to Joyce, Pilla, and Ruiz. He put his hand on my shoulder as a gesture of condolence. It was sincere and meant a great deal to me. You just never know how far a simple act of kindness will go.

The moving stories of the fifty-two men in the ground Reaction Force and the hell they drove through could fill another book and did. Staff Sergeant Jeff Struecker, Pilla's squad leader and a Ranger super-soldier, would basically take charge of the convoy when the chain of command began falling out by attrition. Jeff would one day have a substantial change of direction in his life and become an Army chaplain. In his book *The Road to Unafraid*, Jeff tells the heroic story of his men that day and how he faced fear and found courage in God. Read it. You will be inspired.

In all, Task Force Ranger would lose seventeen men. Our Ranger company lost six. The Delta squadron lost six. The Night Stalkers lost five in the crashes. A sobering lesson of the team concept. Every element lost someone. All players are of equal importance because every element is dependent on the other. Of the 165 of us who went in that day, 78 were wounded. Somali casualties were listed well over a thousand.

The 10th Mountain Division of the QRF lost two men coming in to get us. They are seldom mentioned when it comes to the story of *Black Hawk Down*. But they need to know every one of us at the first crash site were thankful they came. We could not have gotten our wounded comrades back without their help.

"All you got to do is make it out of here alive!
And the rest of your life is gravy. GRAVY!"
(from the movie *Platoon*)

For those of us who survive a tragic event where others did not, we will spend the rest of our lives followed by a strange sense of guilt. We all asked the question, "Why me? Why God, did You let me walk away when men who were three times the soldier I was, did not? Men who deserved to live. Men who should have lived. Men with families, children, and wives. Why was I one of the chosen ones? Why me? What am I supposed to do with this?"

You can do one of two things with the guilt. You can get angry and let the unfairness of it all bury you. Or you can choose to let it motivate you. See it for what it is. It's more than an opportunity or some divine "second chance." See it as a responsibility, a duty, and a commitment to those who got you out of there to carry on and live a happy life filled with purpose, direction, and motivation.

Years later, even after the noise of slamming doors no longer made me duck for cover, and the mere site of Old Glory no longer made me cry, I was still feeling the effects of combat. I was still fighting the Battle of Mogadishu, only now I was years away, safe at home in the middle of a good life.

Guilt continued to haunt me. Sure, I followed my dreams of music. The intestinal fortitude instilled in me as a Ranger would not allow otherwise. Outwardly I was a positive, motivated, dreamer skipping through life doing what I loved to do. Good for me. Way to go.

But down inside I could never fully commit to enjoying the life I had. In fact, I could never fully commit to anything. Why? Because it just didn't seem "hard" enough. Somewhere in my heart, I felt I wasn't supposed to be happy. It should be enough that I was here when others were not.

Guilt affected everything—my sense of self-worth, my relationships, and my ability to enjoy the life God gave me. The moment I felt the good life closing in, the voice of guilt began to whisper. "You know, you're not allowed to be happy. Think about Casey's wife. Think about Pilla's parents. How do you think they feel?"

And so the enemy within me would covertly sabotage whatever good God sent my way. I became a master of disguise, camouflaging my emotions. On the outside I appeared passionate and full of fire, declaring "I love my life. I love you!" Because as a "good Christian," that's what I knew I was supposed to be. In reality, however, I was shutting down my feelings because somewhere between the streets of Mogadishu, the hospitals of recovering friends, and the tombstones at Arlington, I convinced myself I didn't deserve to be here.

It takes one to know one, and it was a Vietnam veteran, a friend of my father, who wrote to me after yet another painful breakup I somehow managed to manufacture. And without talking to me or knowing me all that well, he pinpointed the problem with the accuracy of a laser-guided missile.

"You know, Keni, you are allowed to be happy," he said. "In fact, you owe it to those guys who got you out of there."

Yeah, yeah, tell me something I hadn't already heard.

But it was this next line I remember most that planted the seed of change in my restless and guilt-ridden heart.

"If any one of your friends could come back from the dead and talk to you today, do you really think they would tell you that you were supposed to feel guilty?"

I'm not saying the change was an immediate metamorphosis, as if God Himself spoke the words and then *"shazam!"* I was struck by a bolt of lightning. But the spark was ignited and I knew that combat veteran of Vietnam was right. I'd grown accustomed to the numbness and was comfortable within the walls I erected around my heart. It is exactly those walls we build to protect us that ultimately will imprison us. This guilt I dragged around with me like a ball and chain was self-imposed. I had the key all along.

God indeed spoke to me. The choice was mine to make. It was time to start breaking free of Somalia and begin running out of that city for good.

My good buddy Raleigh Cash who fought through ambush after ambush to come in and get us.

Chapter 10

EXTRAORDINARY INDIVIDUALS

Recognizing I Volunteered as a Ranger,
fully knowing the hazards of my chosen profession.
—1ST STANZA OF THE RANGER CREED

WE'VE ALL HEARD STORIES ABOUT the "ordinary" individual who does the "extraordinary" deed.

A man risks his life to save a woman from an oncoming train in a New York City subway. An office worker jumps into a freezing river to rescue a stranger whose car has gone off a bridge. While her friends spend their summer at the beach, a high school junior uses her vacation to help others by building schools in Central America. A Boy Scout expertly employs the first aid skills he was taught to save a friend from drowning. An inner-city school teacher struggles successfully to inspire and change an entire community.

It doesn't just have to be about combat. Hurricanes. Floods. Earthquakes. Tsunamis. 9/11. Catastrophic events of biblical proportion, we've all watched it happened in this lifetime. And somewhere in the midst of all that devastation there is always an extraordinary story of someone, somewhere doing something heroic. We've seen it in the news. We've read them in *People* magazine. We might even have some of our own.

I, too, have witnessed things on the field of battle that can be described as nothing less than heroic, in the truest sense of the word.

Doc Strous's ability to stay so calm and tend to the wounded under such extreme circumstances saved lives. People with weapons were targeting him specifically, and even when he was hit by shrapnel, he went about his work as if he'd spent every day of his life caring for trauma wounds while being shot at. Just think, a few years before that he was in high school. We were fortunate to have him as our medic. He was extraordinary.

I think about our platoon sergeant, Sergeant First Class Watson, and his ability to orchestrate us through out that chaos and lead us back to safety. His situational awareness and sense of humor created a pillar of confidence everyone around him could rally around. We knew we were in good hands. Do you know every Ranger in our chalk under his direct control made it back alive? Given the circumstances, I find that to be truly extraordinary.

Great leaders are a privilege to those assigned to follow. When you find someone you admire, learn from them. Emulate them. Follow the example they set. Sean T. Watson will always be one such man to me. To this day, I would still follow him anywhere.

And I will never forget the incredible selfless actions of Master Sergeant Gary Gordon and Sergeant First Class Randy Shughart. A couple days after the battle, our platoon was pulled into a briefing room and shown the video footage taken from a reconnaissance aircraft filming the second crash site. As we sat there and watched in silence, an intelligence officer calmly described what we were seeing. He talked like a play-by-play analyst with the insulting detachment of a nightly newscaster. That's because he spent the entire battle in a command center watching the whole scene unfold like some one-dimensional highlight reel on ESPN. For those of us who were out on those streets in full living color— under fire, feeling the fear, and fighting with everything we had to keep each other alive—what we were watching was painfully real.

If you remember, a few minutes after the first Black Hawk was shot down, Super 64, piloted by Michael Durant and Ray Frank, was called in to take over the vacant flight pattern. Moments later they, too, were hit with an RPG and were forced to head back to base. The rocket slammed into the tail. At first, it seemed structurally, the aircraft was holding together and Super 64 would be able to make it back. But the blast did more damage than anyone thought. It didn't take long for the tail rotor, churning away at 1,200 revolutions per minute, to come apart.

With nothing left to counter the main rotors and keep the aircraft straight, the once gravity-defying machine was forced into an irreversible spin. Impact with the ground was eminent. Chief Durant had just enough time to radio their status in typical Night Stalker fashion—matter-of-fact, cool, calm, and collected.

"Six-four is going in. Six-four is going in."

Durant and Frank crashed about a mile away in a shanty town full of shacks, slums, and Somalis hell-bent to kill whatever Americans might still be alive. What moments before was an invincible special operations MH-60 Black Hawk, was now reduced to a collapsed and smoking heap of fuselage only vaguely resembling a helicopter.

There was nobody left to come to their aid. Everyone was already committed to the first crash. A ground convoy was being pieced together and would try to get there. But they weren't going to make it in time.

Master Sergeant Gordon and Sergeant First Class Shughart were Delta snipers aboard Super 62, one of the last remaining helicopters in the air. Their job was to pull security for the guys on the ground. From their vantage point above the city, they could clearly see the scene below going from bad to worse. With the inevitability of an oncoming stampede, hundreds of armed militia and an angry mob of Somalis were racing toward the incapacitated crew. If anyone was going to make it in time to rescue the soldiers who might still be alive, Gordon and Shughart were the only ones in a position to do so.

Gordon called in the situation report stressing the urgency of the situation.

They were denied.

Gordon repeated the request, this time emphasizing that he could see movement inside the wreckage meaning someone was still alive. Somalis were starting to move in.

Denied.

Apparently saving the lives of the survivors was not worth the risk of losing another ten million dollar aircraft and its crew. When you are the guy making those kinds of decisions from the relative safety of a high orbiting command aircraft, I suppose your risk assessment seems logical and justified. But when you are a Delta sniper sitting on the floor of a screaming Black Hawk just a hundred feet above the gunfight where your comrades wait in dire need of help, risk assessment is not something you think about with detached logic. You do what needs to be done right then and there, because someone is counting on you. And if you don't step up, who will?

Fortunately, the man making the big decisions back in the command center was General William Garrison, a leader among men, but a soldier first who understood the heart and mind of the man on the ground. When the ground convoy trying to get to the second crash site was turned back, Garrison was out of options.

Master Sergeant Gordon called for the third time and repeated his request to insert. This time, he was finally given the go.

Michael Goffena was Super 62's pilot and Mike Durant's good friend. Goffena knew the survivors wouldn't last long unless help got there in a hurry. So he picked a spot in an open area where he could put the two snipers in. They would have to run about a hundred yards, but it was as close as he could get.

As Chief Goffena flared to touch down, Super 62 came under heavy attack from small arms fire. Every *tink-tink-tink* on the side of his aircraft meant a few more rounds punctured the thin skin and was wrecking havoc with its mechanical innards. To a helicopter pilot forced to sit tight on the ground while people are shooting, time moves backward. He's thinking, "We gotta go, and we gotta go like yesterday!"

Once Shughart and Gordon were on the deck, Goffena immediately began lifting the Black Hawk out to escape the increasing barrage of bullets. But just like during the initial insertion, the brownout and rotor wash was choking and disorienting. As the big helicopter pulled away, the dirt kicked up like a giant dust devil and neither of the Delta operators was sure which way to move. Shughart signaled up to the pilots asking for the direction of the crash.

Ignoring the *tink-tink-tink* once again, Chief Goffena willingly took his bird back down to the ground to help show the way for the misdirected snipers. He actually pointed out the window to guide the two men. The crew chief even threw out a smoke grenade in the direction of the downed aircraft. The operators gave a thumbs-up as Super 62 once more pulled away to provide covering fire. Taking full responsibility for their own actions, knowing they were astronomically outnumbered and that backup would not be coming any time soon, Gary Gordon and Randy Shughart sprinted headfirst into the storm.

Sgt. First Class Brad Hallings was a third Delta operator aboard Super 62. He stayed with the aircraft so he could provide sniper support for his two comrades on the ground. They were in the air doing just that when an RPG ripped a hole in the left side of the aircraft, forcing Goffena to head back to the airfield. Task Force Ranger lost another Black Hawk. Brad Hallings would lose his leg in the explosion. Shughart and Gordon would lose what little help they had. The two men were on their own.

Under intense small arms fire and with complete disregard for their own safety, Gordon and Shughart fought their way to the wreck of Super 64. One by one, they methodically held off the advancing militia. With steady rhythm and lethal accuracy, they fired round after round after round. Remember, they were Delta operators. They did not miss. This should give you some idea of the numbers they were up against. They fired and fired until there were no more rounds to be fired. With nothing left to protect them, they were overrun and killed. When it was all over, Mike Durant would be the only survivor.

The modern battlefield is not a video game. Weapons run out of ammunition. Men die and do not come back to life.

The Ted Koppel-like intelligence officer showing us the video in the briefing room said something irrelevant like "at this point, indigenous personnel have overrun the crash site."

Indigenous personnel have overrun the crash site? Yeah, well, we can see that, you tool. That's it? That's all you have to say? How about "I'm sorry for the loss of six more of your comrades"? How about "It is an honor to have served in the company of such heroes"?

Those two men put their lives on the line so others might live. Master Sergeant Gary Gordon and Sergeant First Class Randy Shughart would later be honored in history with the Congressional Medal of Honor. When I tell you it is an honor and a privilege to tell the story of Task Force Ranger, I mean it from the bottom of my heart.

Mike Durant was taken captive that day. We got him back eleven days later. His is a story of faith, brotherhood, and perseverance. He will tell you, he owes his life to those two men. Read his book *In the Company of Heroes*. It will inspire you.

Shughart. Gordon. Doc Strous. Sean Watson. Keith Jones. And yes, even David Floyd. They all performed extraordinary deeds and fantastic acts of valor in the most extraordinary circumstances. But don't think for one second any one of them was an "ordinary" individual. They were anything but ordinary. They were exceptional at a time when someone to their left and someone to their right needed them to be. They understood what it meant to be counted on, so they stepped up and did exactly what needed to be done at the precise moment they were needed. This is not ordinary.

Nor should you think for one second anyone who wears the boots and is over there right now in defense of our nation is an ordinary individual. It takes an extraordinary spirit to do what they do, day after day, month after month, year after year. Medals and citations are important to recognize folks for their achievement, but that's not what makes these recipients exceptional people.

What truly sets them apart from the norm is their dedication to excellence in work and character as a life choice. Therein lies the hardest part of wearing the uniform. Getting yourself up every morning and saying, "Today I will better myself. Today I will set the example for others to follow. Today I will shoulder more than my share of the task, whatever it may be, 100 percent and then some." The day-in and day-out commitment to a higher calling where bettering oneself and those around you is a constant endeavor requires the character of an extraordinary person.

"I never had a policy; I have just tried to do my very best each and every day." (Abraham Lincoln)

Certainly we all have it in us to do what must be done when the urgency of a situation requires us to do so. I like to believe human beings are a heroic bunch when it comes down to a pinch. If a car accident were to happen in front of you, I am confident most of you would run to help the victims at the crash. If the roof of your neighbor's house got torn off from a tornado that leveled the town, I bet you would offer your assistance, no questions asked.

When the city of Nashville was devastated by floods, there were no stories of looters and rampant crime. The mayor didn't hold a press conference and whine on national TV that someone else should be doing more to help. What kind of example would that set? Instead of wasting time pointing fingers and assigning blame, the community got to work doing what had to be done. They helped repair the damage, house the homeless, feed the hungry, and gave whatever they could to rebuild Music City. I am proud of my town. I am proud of our citizens. When difficult situations come calling, as they most certainly will, I hope the rest of the nation follows Nashville's strong example of character.

But what about when nothing out of the ordinary is going on, like a meeting at work, a Bible study group at church, a parent-teacher conference at school, or a traffic jam at rush hour? What kind of leadership begs for your attention then? How would you answer the following questions: Am I setting a positive example for others to follow in all I do? Am I using this moment to lead the way?

When you are a person of strong character, the answers are simple. Yes. You know exactly what needs to be done because you understand the burden of leadership. You have dedicated yourself to doing the hard work of continual self-improvement, where you train as you fight, so you will fight as you train. This way, whatever situation is thrown at you, you will be mentally alert, physically strong, and morally straight. These are not the characteristics of an *ordinary* individual.

Ordinary does not do the difficult work required. Ordinary will not go the extra mile. Ordinary is content to say "I *almost* made it." Ordinary does not understand nor accept the responsibility of being counted on. But you do. Please do not buy into the lie that "extraordinary" is for someone else.

As this book approached the end, here's what I ask of you: Never sell yourself short and think you are just an "ordinary" individual. You are anything but. Don't even say it, because if you say it once, you'll say it again. Say it enough and you'll start to believe it. When you start believing something, you'll start to live it. Gradually, you will stop seeking to better yourself because you figure, "What's the point?"

When you stop trying to better yourself, you no longer lead by example. When you no longer lead by example, you stop making a difference. When you stop making a difference, then what are you doing here? You're taking up space, that's what you're doing.

Lead. Follow. Or get out of the way.

Have you ever wondered how some people can stand idly by and do nothing in a situation where someone is in desperate need of help? Do you know why those people choose to do nothing? Because they don't believe they can make a difference. They don't think their input matters. They are afraid of failing.

But you are not that person. You are so much more.

Out of the billions of people on this planet, there is no one else like you. You are one-of-a-kind. God created you as a unique individual, armed and equipped with special gifts to be used for the greater good of you and those around you.

Paul wrote about it in the book of Romans. "In his grace, God has given us different gifts for doing certain things well. So if God has given you the ability to prophesy, speak out with as much faith as God has given you. If your gift is serving others, serve them well. If you are a teacher, teach well. If your gift is to encourage others, be encouraging. If it is giving, give generously. If God has given you leadership ability, take the responsibility seriously. And if you have a gift for showing kindness to others, do it gladly" (Rom. 12:6–8 NLT).

Just like a soldier is assigned basic equipment and task-specific gear to get the job done, you too have everything you need to accomplish your mission. It came wrapped up with the package the day you were brought into this world. But the equipment is only as good as the operator. If you do not learn to use it, a rifle is useless. If you do not continue to train and stay proficient, your skills will erode. So is the case with God's gifts to you.

Will you use them or lose them? Will you seek to improve them? Will you hone and sharpen your skills and use them for bettering the team around you? Of course you will. But remember, you will only be as good as you prepared yourself to be. So how hard are you willing to work?

It's not going to be easy. It's not supposed to be. Struggle and hardship are the building blocks of character. But I have a feeling you already know this.

"Show me a hero and I will write you a tragedy." (F. Scott Fitzgerald)

Maybe you are a single mom with two children to provide for, a career to manage, and a life to live. While your friends all have husbands who share the work load and are there to lean on, being a sole provider is a burden you carry alone. But you drive on and do what must be done. Because if not you, then who? Who else will set the example for your two kids?

Maybe you are a high school senior living at your uncle's house because he's the only one who would take you in when your father disappeared and your mother was put in jail. Every school day you get yourself up, grab your backpack, get it on, and march yourself down to the corner to wait for the city bus to take you to school. On top of the already challenging demands of life as a high school teenager, this extra weight is yours to carry. But who else can do it? Who else will put the building blocks in place for your future if you don't?

Or perhaps you are a dad who's up at 5:30 a.m. and out the door by 6 a.m. to beat the traffic to get to a job that will keep you there until 6 p.m. for you to get home just before 8. Half of your day and half of your life is spent providing. Your work is honest; your ethic is hard. And then one day, as you drop your son off to soccer practice, you get the call. They are without a coach and all the soccer moms are looking at you. They already know what you are thinking. "I know nothing of soccer. I have no time. I'm not ready for this." But if not you, then who else will do it? Who else will lead the way and set an example for others to follow?

As a parent, a teacher, a consultant, a student, an attorney, a manager, social worker, missionary, a sister, brother, soldier, sailor, airman, or marine, it's going to get tough. You knew that going in. Being tired, busy, overworked, and having many responsibilities can seem like legitimate challenges, especially in addition to the demands of everyday life, but these are all part of the burden of leadership. And many times you will carry these burdens alone.

No calling, no job, no government, and no way of life comes with a 100 percent guarantee. We are guaranteed only the *pursuit* of happiness, not necessarily the end result. It may not always work out the way we want it to. But we drive on and do what must be done because we know there are people counting on us to do so. We do the right thing because it's the right thing to do. That's what it means to lead the way.

Every single story I can tell you about triumph and great achievement came with a price. Where would we be as a nation, if not for the likes of men like Casey Joyce, Dominick Pilla, Lorenzo Ruiz, Gary Gordon, and Randy Shughart? In the words of my friend Stan Wood, *Gunslinger's* pilot, "All these guys shaped the way we fight today." But those invaluable lessons learned came at a cost no one wanted to pay.

"I am well aware of the toil and blood and treasure that it will cost to maintain this Declaration, and support and defend these States. Yet through all the gloom I can see the rays of ravishing light and glory. I can see that the end is worth more than the means." (John Quincy Adams on the Declaration of Independence in a letter to his wife Abigail)

Every morning at 0 dark 30, somewhere in the world, a group of Rangers are standing in formation. They are called to attention. The First Sergeant asks for "six motivated individuals" to recite the Ranger Creed. If you are a private, you better beat your team leader up there or there will be hell to pay.

There is a mad scramble out of the ranks as volunteer's race to the front. The first six to get there line up at the position of attention. Each man then recites one stanza out of six that make up the Ranger Creed and the entire company repeats it back. It begins like this:

"Recognizing I volunteered as a Ranger . . ."

And the Rangers repeat, "Recognizing I volunteered as a Ranger . . ."

Gary Gordon and Randy Shughart knew exactly what they volunteered for when they made their request to be inserted. There was an overwhelming force of armed men clearly en route. But that came with the territory. That is what they signed up to do.

Gary's wife Carmen knew without a doubt why her husband volunteered to do what no one in their right mind would have done. "Gary was 100 percent Ranger. He lived the Ranger Creed. He went in there to help his fellow soldiers. Not to die."

". . . Fully knowing the hazards of my chosen profession."

And the Rangers repeat, "Fully knowing the hazards of my chosen profession."

Can you imagine if at home, or at your job, or in your school, you had a creed that you and your family or colleagues recite before the day begins? Something motivating that will inspire in you the will to fight for a cause that is bigger than yourself. A mission statement with a purpose to remind you why you are there and just how important you are. A testament that provides direction and screams to the world, "This is who I am and this is where I am going. Follow me!"

Imagine lining up your family, coworkers, classmates, or staff first thing in the morning and as a highly-motivated individual, standing tall in front of them and shouting, "Recognizing I volunteered as a (*insert your current calling in life here*) fully knowing the hazards of my chosen profession!"

The point of saying a creed everyday is to make it more than a bunch of words. You say it enough, you begin to believe it. You begin to believe it and you will start living it. I don't know if you have a creed to live by. A prayer, an oath, a pledge, or a solemn promise you repeat on a daily basis. Something that reminds you to be there for those you lead 100 percent and then some. But if you need one, I've got one for you.

It's on the walls of the 75th Ranger Regiment. It's on the walls of the Delta compound in Fort Bragg, North Carolina. It's on the walls of the 160th Special Operations Air Regiment, the SEAL Team locker rooms, and the Air Force special operations command in Tampa, Florida. In fact, it's on the walls of every single one of our special operations unit out there. It's from the Bible, and it's found in Isaiah 6:8.

> "Then I heard the voice of the Lord saying, 'Whom shall I send? And who will go for us? And I said, 'Here am I. Send me.'" (NIV)

I used to think that was strictly a military verse. Cool! Isaiah wrote a Scripture just for the soldier. "Send me" was an easy thing for us to say. It was not our job to ask why, ours was *"but to do or die."* We were the charging light brigade. We sang about it. We trained for it. We lived for it. We needed to know if we were ready for it. Please somebody, anybody, start a war.

But you know what? Out of the thirty-two references to soldiers in the Bible, Isaiah 6:8 is not included as one of them. That's because Isaiah had a bigger audience in mind than just the fighting man.

I don't get to wear the uniform of the 75th Ranger Regiment anymore. I don't get to stand shoulder to shoulder and hold the line with the greatest men this country has ever known. I no longer carry a rifle. But I do get to carry a guitar. Both have a working end. Both can make an impact. My mission is no longer raids and reconnaissance. But you can still send me. I can sing a song. I can tell a story. These are the gifts I have been given. And you can count on me to use them to the absolute best of my ability.

I could never know all that is required of you in your chosen calling or profession. But I do know that whatever it is you do, you are better equipped for it than I am. This is why to every audience I get a chance to speak to, I thank them. "Thank you for raising your hand. Thank you for doing something that I cannot and what most others aren't willing to try. You are the heroes and you are the saints. You have been sent."

But remember this. Once you step forward and say "Send me. Give me the job. Give me the responsibility. You can count on me 100 percent and then some," you have now become part of something much larger than yourself. You have become part of a thing called a team, where someone to your left and to your right are always counting on you.

You are anything but ordinary. You are the one piece of the puzzle that makes everything work. You have everything you need to accept the challenges that others shy away from. Your character is rock-solid and your faith is strong. God is on your side. So drive on to the Ranger objective and complete the mission though you be the lone survivor. Push forward in the face of adversity while shouting out to those around you "Follow Me." Lead the way with purpose, direction, and motivation even if the only person you are leading is yourself.

"To every man there comes in his lifetime that special moment when he is tapped on the shoulder and offered the chance to do a very special thing, unique to him and fitted to his talents. What a tragedy if that moment finds him unprepared and unqualified for the work which would be his finest hour." (Winston Churchill)

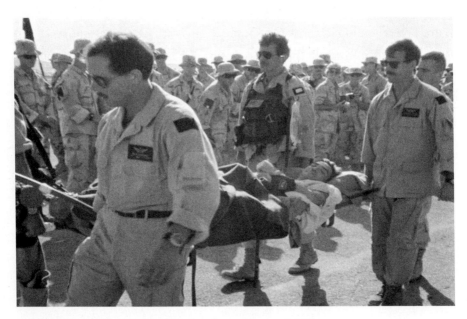

The day we got Mike Durant back after eleven days as a POW.

Chapter 11

RLTW

Rangers Lead the Way!
—6TH STANZA OF THE RANGER CREED

THE MOST LASTING LESSON I learned from my years in the Rangers came on the very first day I walked into the 3rd Ranger Battalion in Fort Benning, Georgia. The Command Sergeant Major of the entire Ranger Regiment Leon-Guerrero was a legendary Ranger and was there to greet us. "LG" was a short stocky man from Guam who spoke with the fierce terseness of a Samurai warrior.

"Men!" he said, "I want to congratulate you all for choosing to do something with your lives that is an *honorable* and *noble* profession!" Like a hammer coming down, he slammed his fist into his other hand to accentuate the significance of these words.

I was a know-it-all kid out of college who thought I'd seen a thing or two, but I had no idea what the words "honorable and noble" meant. For me they were simply overly dramatic punch lines used in movies and words reserved for long-ago heroes named Lancelot and Audie Murphy.

The sergeant major continued with his "sermon" using unfamiliar language like ideology, creeds, and dedication. He stressed the importance of the Ranger buddy concept. Taking care of each other begins by taking care of yourselves. He went on to boldly tell us that from that day forth, our lives would never be the same. We would become better people for the experience and hopefully the world would be a better place as a result.

"Some of you will become part of the long and colorful history of this Ranger Regiment. Some of you will go on to lengthy and distinguished careers in the military. Most of you will do your time, get out and go back into the real world. But wherever it is you go, remember what you learn here."

Again the sergeant major pounded his fist on the *Ranger* downbeat to make his point.

"The world needs *Ranger* Doctors! And *Ranger* Lawyers! And *Ranger* teachers! Rangers Lead the Way!" With that, he turned and left the room.

I used to think it was simply something we were required to say to an officer as you saluted him.

"Rangers lead the way, sir."

He would return your salute and reply accordingly "all the way."

This salute was so much more than a motto or some boys club, frat house, exclusive, secret, meet-and-greet formality. It was a reminder and a homage to the sacrifice and commitment made by all those thousands of rangers past, present, and future. Wear that scroll on your shoulder and you are expected and counted on to lead the way in all you do.

From the beaches of Normandy and the Burmese jungles, to the mountains of Keisan and the rice paddies of Vietnam. Grenada, Panama, Desert Storm, Somalia, Iraq, Afghanistan, and all the places you never hear about, the history of the Rangers is a long and colorful one. Many men have died leading the way on the field of battle. Many more will. For those of us left to carry on here in the real world, we must take what we learned from those experiences and spread the word. I know now what Command Sergeant Major "LG" was telling us all those years ago on that very first day.

The world needs leaders. "Ranger doctors. Ranger lawyers. And Ranger teachers." Sure, your job and your coworkers need you to lead by example. But so does your family. Your community. Your church. Lord knows this nation needs great leaders. The world needs people of character. The world needs you.

"Be who you are and say what you feel, because those who mind don't matter and those who matter don't mind." (Dr. Seuss)

Nowadays I get to travel the country and the world telling stories. Be it through lyric and melody playing at a forward operating base in northern Afghanistan or standing on a stage giving a speech to a thousand educators in California, my mission right now is clear to me. Do what I love to do and lead the way while doing it. It is a privilege, an honor, and a huge blessing.

It's a blessing because I'm doing exactly what I love to do in a manner in which only I can do it. As an entertainer on numerous USO tours with the Sergeant Major of the Army, I've gone places most artists never knew existed. I was asked to sing our national anthem at Yankee Stadium for game one of the World Series. The Yankees could have asked anyone. They chose me. I've sung side by side with superstars I admire like Kenny Rogers, Vince Gill, Emmylou Harris, and Michael McDonald. They all volunteered to sing on my record because it benefited the families of our fallen military personnel. I've even been invited to perform on the Grand Ole Opry during several of their special tributes to the troops.

Being a veteran and a storyteller with a guitar has taken me places I never dreamed of and introduced me to people I could never have had access to as a soldier. I've met with generals, admirals and secretaries of defense. Governors, mayors, CEOs and celebrities. I've gotten to talk with two presidents and sang at another's inauguration. I have traveled to every state in our nation and shaken hands with thousands. I've met the left. I've met the right. I've been to the North and to the South. I have met America.

Of all those folks it has been my privilege to get to know, my absolute favorite Americans to spend my time with are still the men and women of our armed forces.

There is no place I would rather be on Christmas Eve than with the USO on a cold makeshift stage somewhere in Afghanistan playing for those fine folks serving our nation. I can think of nothing I would rather do on the Fourth of July than to sing patriotic songs with my band at a Navy base in San Diego. If there is a better place to perform on Memorial Day than the Vietnam Wall, I still haven't found it. But if there is, please let me know because I'd like to sing there too.

Every single one of those doors opened was in some way connected to my prior military service and my status as a combat veteran.

None of it could have ever been possible without God's grace and the men on my left and right who fought to bring me home and get me where I am today. I am indebted to my Ranger brothers.

"From this day to the ending of the world,
But we in it shall be remembered;
We few, we happy few, we band of brothers;
For he today that sheds his blood with me
Shall be my brother." (Shakespeare, Henry V)

The story of Black Hawk Down has been told many times and in many ways. There are several books, a movie, documentaries, and even a video game. There are also a few of us out there who still get invited to speak to audiences and tell the story from a personal perspective.

My friend Matt "the Rat" Eversmann was the chalk leader for Casey Joyce and Todd Blackburn, the young private who fell out of the helicopter during insertion. Matt will give you an inspiring recount of what it was like for him and his men during their piece of the battle.

Danny McKnight was the 3rd Ranger Battalion's commanding officer and was wounded as part of the ground convoy trying to reach the first crash site. His perspective is uniquely sighted from a commander's point of view.

Mike Durant was the pilot of Super 61. When the Somali insurgents overran his crash site, Chief Durant was taken captive and held as a POW for eleven days until we finally got him back. Mike Durant's story of faith in God and his Task Force Ranger brothers can only be told by Mike Durant.

And Jeff Struecker, the Ranger super-soldier squad leader, who lead his men back out into the fight despite their fears is still inspiring soldiers and military families within the Special Operations Community. Jeff found his calling as an Army chaplain. He became an officer and spent the rest of his military career providing purpose, direction, and motivation as a chaplain for the 75th Ranger Regiment. Major Struecker will probably be the only Ranger-tabbed, SCUBA/HALO qualified and three-time combat veteran preacher the chaplain corps has ever known. They will never find another like him.

In fact, it was Jeff who was a pivotal player in guiding my current career. I don't know if Jeff can sing his way out of a wet paper bag, but he sure made an impact on my music. I had been in Nashville for a couple years pursuing my music career and was just about ready to give up. Nothing was happening as fast as I thought it should or expected it to. The war in Iraq was all ahead full steam and I felt guilty for not being a part of it. I was still fully capable of carrying a weapon and leading men in uniform. As the possessor of a unique skill set well suited for the mission in Iraq, I was offered a job by one of the contracting companies doing combat-related work in country. I accepted the offer and was ready to leave my dreams of music behind. And then God showed up, again.

This time He came speaking through an old friend. Jeff called me up one day out of the blue and wasted no time getting straight to the point with a conversation that changed the course of my life.

"Hey, Keni, I heard you were coming back in and heading over to Iraq."

I told him about my reasoning as he listened and said he understood.

"I understand why you want to come back in. And yes we could use you over there. But if you don't mind me saying so, I'm calling to tell you why I think you should *not* come back in."

He went on to explain to me about gifts and talents, callings and responsibilities to do what God has called you to do.

He said, "Keni, you know as well as I do we can train someone up to be a great soldier. But I don't know anyone who can do what you do. Whether you know it or not, you are the voice of the Rangers right now. We see you on the documentaries and you make us proud. I'm praying for your music career to bust wide open because you have the ability to do more with one song than I can do with a year's worth of sermons."

Whoa. When a preacher calls you out of the blue and tells you to do something, you better start listening. Short of a burning bush, I'm not sure God could have spoken any more directly to me. I thanked Jeff. Turned down the job offer in Iraq. And prayed God would guide me if I stayed the course and stuck with the music.

Three months later I signed my first record deal. And later that year we recorded an incredible album called *Flags of Our Fathers* the proceeds of which would eventually help benefit the children of our special operations warriors killed in combat or training. (Please see the Special Operations Warrior Foundation.) Our first single off that album "Not Me" was an unexpected hit and put me on the map as an up-and-coming country music artist.

If you think God is not watching out for you, you are mistaken. Better still, if you want to know He is there, all you have to do is ask. You'll be amazed at how quickly He shows up.

"Ask and it will be given to you; seek and you will find." (Matthew 7:7)

Jeff Struecker is a powerful speaker. As a combat veteran with a CIB, he is in a unique position to use his experience in the Battle of Mogadishu as a stepping-stone to help spread the gospel. As a POW Mike Durant is the only person who can tell the story of Mike Durant and the faith he clung to in God and his Task Force Ranger brothers. Danny McKnight, Matt Eversmann, and even Mark Bowden can tell you all about their take on the battle, and each story would be time well spent by you.

But as good as they are, none of those men who are handed a mic and asked to talk about Task Force Ranger can tell you about David Floyd, Eric Suranski, Randy Ramaglia, Melvin Dejesus, Sean T. Watson, Peter Neathery, or Doc Strous. Not the way I can. It is my story to tell and only I can tell it as Keni Thomas would. So to all who will listen, you can send me. It is an honor to do so because I know that by the grace of God the only reason I'm still here today doing what I love is because of those men. And if I don't tell their story, who will?

A couple days after the battle, General Garrison called me into his office in a trailer across from the airplane hangar. There was going to be a press conference, and I was one of the enlisted men selected to be on the panel. By now the world knew about the battle and had seen the ugly images of American bodies being drug through the streets by a celebrating Somali mob. Like a bunch of ambulance-chasing injury attorneys, the previously disinterested press was now eager to talk to us. I was told the General wanted to brief me on what I could and couldn't talk about. But that isn't at all what General Garrison wanted to talk about.

"Sergeant Thomas, how are your men?"

That was his first concern. I spent a little time bragging about Suranski, Floyd, and Dejesus as he chewed on his signature cigar and listened. I even fulfilled a promise to Suranski and asked the general if the Army would create a combat fast rope award. He just gnawed and smiled. I took that as a no. And then General Garrison said what he had called me in there to say, what he wanted to say to the world but instead would pass the message on through one of his young sergeants.

"Sergeant Thomas, you make sure you tell them how magnificently your men performed here."

Like a wise old Yoda, General William Garrison could already foresee what was coming. The finger pointing. The blaming. The cowardice of a new administration ducking the questions of "how could this happen?" He didn't want the memory of Task Force Ranger to be so tainted by political fallout that what was really important and historically significant was overlooked.

William Garrison was a leader of men and a soldier's soldier. He started as an enlisted man during the Vietnam War, got a battlefield commission, and eventually worked his way up to the higher echelons of special operations. He understood the heart of the fighting man. So what mattered most to him was not how this might affect his career. Nor was he concerned with the weak opinions of the armchair quarterbacking pencil-necked policy makers. What he cared about was making certain the world recognized the warriors who fought the fight and made their nation proud.

"Ours was a great victory, and history should remember it as such," he told me.

On my wall today there hangs only one military plaque. It was given to me by Sergeant First Class Watson and the men of 3rd platoon the day I left the 3rd Ranger battalion and took a new job with the 75th Ranger Reconnaissance Detachment. It is inscribed with some motivating words from Teddy Roosevelt. I wished I had known about this quote the day General Garrison sent me into that press conference. I would have read it to the folks in attendance, got up, and walked out.

"It is not the critic who counts; not the man who points out how the strong man stumbles, or where the doer of deeds could have done them better. The credit belongs to the man who is actually in the arena, whose face is marred by dust and sweat and blood, who strives valiantly; . . . who knows the great enthusiasm, the great devotion, who spends himself in a worthy cause, who at the best knows in the end the triumph of high achievement and who at the worst, if he fails, at least he fails while daring greatly. So that his place shall never be with those cold and timid souls who know neither victory nor defeat." (Theodore Roosevelt)

I took General Garrison's words to heart and have since done my best to use every opportunity I get to make sure the world knows how magnificently my men performed that day.

When we returned to Fort Benning, I wrote my guys up for an award. Despite the "we're too hard for awards" attitude and the "we were just doing our job" Ranger mentality, I felt the recognition was important. Floyd and Suranski were awarded the Army Commendation Medal distinguished with a V device for their valorous service during combat operations. Specialist Melvin Dejesus was awarded the Bronze Star for his meritorious service and superb execution of his job as a SAW gunner and team leader. I'm not sure if "everyone in Puerto Rico has a Bronze Star" but I hope the Roach uses it to tell the story when his peers ask him "hey, what did you get that for?"

I also wrote citation recommendations for Specialist Richard Strous, Sergeant Randy Ramaglia, and Sergeant First Class Sean T. Watson. All were awarded the Bronze star with a "V" device for valor which distinguishes the award for an act of combat heroism. I gave mine to my mom. It hangs in a frame as you walk in her door. She will proudly tell you about it whether you ask her or not.

In total, Task Force Ranger would become one of the most decorated battalions in military history. Two Congressional Medals of Honor to Randy Shugart and Gary Gordon. Tim Wilkinson, the likeable Air Force PJ who risked his life several times to save others, was presented with the Air Force Cross, the second highest honor the Air Force can bestow.

The Night Stalkers had five Distinguished Flying Cross recipients in recognition of their "extraordinary heroism." Just to put that in perspectives, that's the same award our country gave Charles Lindbergh for flying across the Atlantic. And according to the Army Awards Department over three dozen Silver Stars requiring presidential approval were authorized to include all the Navy SEALs.

For the TFR vets who remained in uniform and made a career of it, like Jim Lechner and Jeff Struecker or the ones like Raleigh Cash, Mike Goodale, and me who got out and went back into "the real world," the awards of cloth and tin we wore on our uniforms or hang in a frame will forever serve as a reminder that we are part of something much larger than ourselves. We are all a part of the long and colorful history of the Ranger Regiment. It is our duty to carry on by taking what we learned there and to "gallantly show the world" what is means to lead the way.

"The war is over for me now. But it will always be here for the rest of my days. For those of us who did make it, we have an obligation to teach others what we know and to try with what's left of our lives to find a goodness and meaning to this life." (Oliver Stone from the movie *Platoon*)

All of us want to make a difference. We all want to know at the end of the day we counted for something. I know you do. It's why you get up everyday and go to work doing whatever it is you do, working a job, raising a child, going to school, or volunteering your time. To the men and women in uniform reading this book, making a difference is not something you have to worry about. It came with your standard issue.

But for the rest of us out here living day to day, we struggle with the how. How do I matter? How will I count? How will I make a difference?

The answer is easy. You do what Floyd did. You do what Suranski did. You do what Dejesus and every other member of Task Force Ranger did out there in the streets of Mogadishu. You lead. And you lead by example. Because when you set an example for others to follow, the folks around you become better for it and the team is stronger. They may not pat you on the back or give you an award. But they will have noticed and find inspiration in the example you set. You then have made a difference. And just like Leroy the WW II veteran, "Grandfather, Optimist, and Dreamer" taught me, you never know how far a little positivity will go.

While the answer may be easy, the hard work of leading is not. You will be called upon to rise above yourself and do what others can not do for you. Your character will be tested. Your faith will be tested. And it's how well you prepared yourself in advance that will be the difference between mission success and mission failure.

Please do not make the naïve mistake of assuming that just because it's quiet, the enemy is not out there. The mere absence of war is not peace. Just like the special operations operator who patrols the mountains of Afghanistan, the rooftops of Iraq, and the dark places around the globe, ready to visit violence on those who would harm us, you too must stay alert and be prepared. "The kingdom of heaven suffers violence" (Matt. 11:12 NASB).

We are all in a fight whether we want to admit it or not. We were born into a world at war. From the moment you were drafted into service on this earth, there was good and there was bad. One is trying to save you. The other is trying to destroy you. Paul gave us the warning order. He wasn't talking about the Romans, Muslim insurgents, or Somali Sunni clan fighters.

"We are not fighting against flesh-and-blood enemies, but against evil rulers and authorities of the unseen world, against mighty powers in this dark world, and against evil spirits in the heavenly places." (Ephesians 6:12 NLT)

Spiritual warfare is real, as real as any conflict ever fought on this earth. The lessons from the battlefield are the same. To fight the good fight and emerge victoriously, it will take training, planning, and strong leadership. The good news is you are never alone in your trials. You have surrounded yourself with good people of strong character and God is on your side. You already have everything you need to not only survive, but to lead the way and to "find goodness and meaning in this life."

I can't tell you when and I can't tell you where. But I can tell you with absolute certainty that the call *will* come and just like that, the course of your life will change forever.

"Put on all of God's armor so that you will be able to stand firm against all strategies of the devil" (Ephesians 6:11 NLT)

Get it on!

> "We do the right thing because it's the right thing to do. That's what it means to lead the way.
> (Tom DiTomasso)

We put up a memorial to the fallen outside of the airplane hangar. At the time, all the bodies had not yet been recovered, which explains why there's only eleven pairs of boots.

THE RANGER CREED

Recognizing that I volunteered as a Ranger, fully knowing the hazards of my chosen profession,

I will always endeavor to uphold the prestige, honor, and high esprit de corps of the Rangers.

Acknowledging the fact that a Ranger is a more elite soldier who arrives at the cutting edge of battle by land, sea, or air,

I accept the fact that as a Ranger my country expects me to move further, faster and fight harder than any other soldier.

Never shall I fail my comrades. I will always keep myself mentally alert, physically strong and morally straight.

I will shoulder more than my share of the task whatever it may be, one-hundred-percent and then some.

Gallantly will I show the world that I am a specially selected and well-trained soldier.

My courtesy to superior officers, neatness of dress and care of equipment shall set the example for others to follow.

Energetically will I meet the enemies of my country. I shall defeat them on the field of battle for I am better trained and will fight with all my might. Surrender is not a Ranger word.

I will never leave a fallen comrade to fall into the hands of the enemy and under no circumstances will I ever embarrass my country.

Readily will I display the intestinal fortitude required to fight on to the Ranger objective and complete the mission though I be the lone survivor.

Rangers Lead the Way!

If you would like to order additional signed copies of *Get it On!* you can order today at

premierecollectibles.com

THANK YOU

FOR PURCHASING *GET IT ON!*

MY GIFT TO YOU:
Music, a free download from my new album Give it Away.

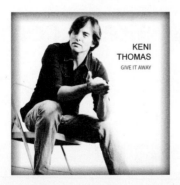

KENI THOMAS
GIVE IT AWAY

Simply go to **kenithomas.com/music** and download it now. And please stay in touch by letting me know what you think. I'm easy to find. I hope you enjoy the book and the music!

If you were moved by this book, you should hear Keni in person!

To find out more about booking Keni for a speaking event visit

premierespeakers.com

I am a long time supporter of

SPECIAL OPERATIONS WARRIOR FOUNDATION

They provide college educations to the children of our special operations personnel killed in training or combat.

To find out more information or to make a donation please visit

specialops.org